Using the
Celtic Cross
to Unveil Your
Hidden Story

photo ©Katherine Kenner

About the Author

Corrine Kenner specializes in bringing metaphysical subjects down to earth. Her work on the tarot is widely published, and her tarot classes and workshops are perennial favorites among students in the Midwest.

Corrine is a certified tarot master, and she has studied tarot under the auspices of the Tarot School of New York, the Wanless Tarot Institute, and Builders of the Adytum. She also holds a bachelor's degree in philosophy from California State University, Long Beach.

Corrine has lived in Brazil, Los Angeles, and the Twin Cities of Minnesota. She now lives in the Midwest with her husband, Dan Horon, and her daughters, Katherine, Emily, and Julia. In her everyday life, she is the vice president and communications director of Cadgraphics Incorporated, a software company that specializes in fire alarm and security systems.

Corrine is the author of Llewellyn's *Tall Dark Stranger*, a guide to using tarot cards for romance, as well as *Crystals for Beginners*. She wrote *The Epicurean Tarot*, published by U.S. Games Systems, Inc., and she was the creator of Llewellyn's *Tarot Calendar*. A former newspaper reporter and magazine editor, Corrine was also the editor of Llewellyn's popular *Astrological Calendar*, *Daily Planetary Guide*, and *Sun Sign Book*, as well as an anthology of supernatural accounts called *Strange But True*.

Corrine Kenner

Tarot journaling

Using the
Celtic Cross
to Unveil Your
Hidden Story

Llewellyn Publications • Woodbury, Minnesota

FIRST EDITION
First Printing, 2006

Book design and editing by Rebecca Zins
Cover design by Lisa Novak
Tarot cards on page 90 from *Universal Tarot* by
Roberto De Angelis; used by permission of Lo Scarabeo

Llewellyn is a registered trademark of Llewellyn Worldwide, Ltd.

Library of Congress Cataloging-in-Publication Data
Kenner, Corrine, 1964–.
    Tarot journaling: using the Celtic cross to unveil your hidden story / Corrine Kenner. —
1st ed.
        p.   cm.
Includes bibliographical references (p.).
    ISBN-13: 978-0-7387-0643-6
    ISBN-10: 0-7387-0643-4
        1. Tarot. 2. Diaries—Authorship—Miscellanea. I. Title.

BF1879.T2K47 2006
133.3'2424—dc22

                                2005044540

Llewellyn Publications
A Division of Llewellyn Worldwide, Ltd.
2143 Woodvale Drive, Dept. 0-7387-0643-4
Woodbury, MN 55125-2989
www.llewellyn.com

Printed in the United States of America

Each new day is a blank page in the diary of your life. The secret of success is in turning that diary into the best story you possibly can.

—DOUGLAS PAGELS

A Cautionary Note

Keeping a tarot journal can be therapeutic, but it isn't therapy. This book was written as a means to help you learn more about yourself, learn more about tarot cards, and have fun. It was not designed to replace the services of a licensed physician or counselor. If you find that the suggestions make you feel uncontrollably weepy, giggly, angry, or outspoken, you may want to seek professional help—or start over with a new journal.

The author and the publisher assume no responsibility for any adverse consequences that may result from the use of this guide, including but not limited to writer's cramp, bad handwriting, or a compulsion to buy blank books, tarot decks, and pens.

Contents

Dedication

To my old *Artist's Way* group in St. Paul: Karen Failes, Lynn Johnson, Kim Labuz, Linda Nicosia, and especially Mary Lynch.

To my tarot friends from the Readers Studio in New York: Wald and Ruth Ann Amberstone, Kim Arnold, Chris Asselin, Joanna Powell Colbert, Jeffrey Elliott, Mark McElroy, Elinor Greenberg, Carolyn Guss, Debbie Lake, Rachel Nguyen, Kevin Quigley, Gina Thies, James Wells, Diane Wilkes, and especially my roommate, Cheryl Sigler.

To the people who encouraged me and helped teach me how to write: Sister Mary Margaret, my seventh- and eighth-grade English teacher; Sam Johnson, my high school journalism instructor; and Catherine Gaugh, my editor at *The Orange County Register*.

And of course, to my husband, Dan Horon; my parents, Wayne and Carolyn Kenner; and my daughters, Katherine, Emily, and Julia.

Foreword

Tarot and psychotherapy are becoming more alike every day. Although most of us start tarot because we want to learn the art of divination, after learning the basics many of us turn to the cards in order to learn more about ourselves. Tarot journaling is an outgrowth of that desire. It allows us to use our fascination with the cards as a vehicle for moving beyond our own surface identity into deeper and more hidden parts of our personality.

As a psychotherapist, I often suggest that my clients keep a therapy journal as a way of keeping them involved in the therapy process between sessions. I encourage them to keep track of their dreams, write about their reactions to their therapy sessions, and jot down any new thoughts and observations that they would like to discuss. Eventually it becomes an emotional autobiography that chronicles their deepest and most personal reactions to their everyday life.

One of the interesting facts about these journals is that many of my clients who successfully keep therapy journals had previously seen themselves as writing failures. Some even had writing phobias that interfered with them turning in papers in college. I could identify with these problems because I had experienced similar difficulties during college myself.

Despite my later success in keeping dream and tarot journals, I initially made a number of failed attempts at keeping a diary. When faced with a blank page and the mission of saying something important about my life on a daily basis, I could not do it. I found it too difficult to access my feelings and get beyond keeping a superficial record of my daily activities. I also was inhibited by my fear that if I wrote truthfully, my parents, roommate, or boyfriend of the time would peek.

As I tried to understand what had changed for my clients and myself that allowed us to keep dream and therapy journals successfully, I realized that the nature of these journals frees us from three things that often get in the way: one, we no longer had to decide what to write about; two, the assigned theme helps us organize our thoughts; and three, we know that the quality of our writing will not be judged—we can jot down a few ideas, write endless run-on sentences, and it does not matter.

Tarot journals share exactly the same virtues. The tarot journal revolves around tarot cards: what they mean, what they look like, our reactions to them, and exercises involving them. This saves us from looking at a blank page and wondering what to write about. In addition, we know from the beginning that the journal is for ourselves and, as Corrine makes abundantly clear in this book, we are free to do anything that we wish with it. We can write in it every day or only occasionally. It can be decorated or plain. There is no right way or wrong way of doing it. What this means is that tarot journals, in addition to teaching the tarot enthusiast more about tarot, allow many of us to experience for the first time the pleasures of journaling.

This new freedom to write can be a heady experience. I went from keeping no journals in high school and college to, at last count, keeping five different types of tarot journals. I began my tarot studies by placing a card in the middle of a blank journal page and writing all my associations to it. Next, as I progressed, I began a journal in which I recorded every reading that I did and which books I used as references. As I grew more confident about my reading skill, I convinced my husband that he should join me in choosing a card a day for each of us, and I recorded my observations about how the card related to what happened to us during the day. Now, whenever I read an interesting book on tarot or begin a new tarot course, I keep a journal at my side to jot down new information, my reactions, and a record of tarot exercises. (Mary Greer and Tom Little's book on court cards, *Understanding the Tarot Court*, inspired my most recent journal of this kind.)

There is another important way that tarot journaling resembles psychotherapy. It helps us access parts of ourselves that may be outside our everyday consciousness. The late Milton H. Erickson, MD, who was arguably the most effective and innovative hypnotherapist of all time, often said that we already have all the tools that we will ever need inside us; hypnosis just helps us access them. From this point of view, the tarot deck is an illustrated compilation of potential tools. All seventy-eight tarot cards represent aspects of the self that exist inside each of us as potential behaviors, talents, and attitudes. Tarot journaling gives us a way to access them and integrate them into our conscious sense of who we are.

This is very similar to what I believe about dreams. As a Gestalt therapist, I believe that all the characters that populate our dreams, no matter how admirable or repugnant, represent parts of us. If we want to get to know our real self better, we have to acknowledge and get to know them. Doing so helps us expand and deepen our sense of who we really are and makes us more integrated and three-dimensional.

Many of us first encounter these other part-selves in dreams. Sometimes they are the monsters that we are fleeing from in nightmares—what Carl Gustav Jung, the great Swiss analyst, called our "shadow" side. Other times they are more benign figures that are based on people we know from everyday life. Whether good, bad, or neutral, on a deeper level they are symbols that represent parts of us. However, it is hard to capture and examine our dreams. By the time we awaken, important details are already lost.

Unlike dreams, tarot has the virtue of being a mirror that we can hold in our hands and look at whenever we want. All we have to do in order to study one of our part-selves is to remove that card from our deck and put it down in front of us. If we wish to, we can use our mind's unconscious responses to the symbols in the card to consciously evoke in ourselves the qualities of that card. The card, in that case, becomes a picture of an intention.

Let me give you an example. Imagine that you are trying to decide what type of tarot journal to keep. You draw a card from your deck for guidance and get the Eight of Cups from the Rider-Waite-Smith deck. As you contemplate the card, you decide that you will let the number of the card direct you to the corresponding chapter in this book, chapter 8: "Your House," and you decide to choose your journal from one of the types described in that chapter. The card's suit, cups, which represents the element of water, suggests to you that you should take an imaginative and emotional approach to your journal.

You gaze at the red-cloaked figure in the Eight of Cups, who appears to be setting out alone to search for his or her heart's desire, and you allow this image to work on your unconscious mind and activate something within you. The Eight of Cups then becomes a picture of your intention to go on your own journey and find within this tarot journal something deeply meaningful and fulfilling for yourself, something new that you don't already have. As you look at the card and think of the theme of family and friends, you might ask yourself: Where am I going? What kind of home did I come from? What type of friends am I seeking? What am I willing to leave behind? If you choose to, you could further deepen the card's association with your new journal by making a copy of the card and attaching it to the journal's cover or first page. You now have invoked its spirit as your guide.

The ease with which tarot can be used to help us move out of our everyday consciousness into something more profound is contributing to the phenomenal growth of tarot today. When we combine the magic of tarot with the introspective nature of keeping a journal, we find ourselves with a powerful tool for personal growth. Whenever we begin a tarot journal, we are knowingly or unknowingly committing to studying and evolving ourselves.

ELINOR GREENBERG, PH.D., is a licensed psychologist and certified professional tarot reader who has been practicing psychotherapy for over thirty years. Dr. Greenberg is psychology consultant to The Tarot School, the holder of a Second Degree from The Tarot School, and is currently working on and writing about how to integrate tarot with psychotherapy. Her article "Tarot Counseling" will appear in *Llewellyn's Tarot Reader 2007.*

Preface: Reading and Writing

I remember the moment when psychologist Jane Alexander Stewart and I laid down the twenty-two oversized cards of the Major Arcana of the tarot, saying to those who had assembled with us, "These are the stations of the journey." Suddenly, we were both in sacred space and in story . . .

—DEENA METZGER,
Writing for Your Life

If you have ever had a tarot card reading—or if you have ever read the cards for somebody else—you know the power and the drama of the cards.

Think back to your time at the tarot reader's table. As the reader shuffled the deck, you might have caught a glimpse of a recognizable image or two: the Lovers, perhaps, or the Wheel of Fortune. Each glance heightened the suspense, and hinted at the tales and the truths that were about to unfold.

As the reading began, each facet of your life came sharply into focus. Your past, present, and future were laid out in front of you. Your foundation was displayed at your feet; your highest ideals were poised directly overhead. Your self-image, your public image, and your hopes and fears were all there to be revealed. Did you embrace the outcome or seek a new course for the future?

People read tarot cards for a variety of reasons. Some are captivated by the illustrations. Some are fascinated by the myths and legends associated with each card. Some want to relive the past, while others want to enjoy and experience the present more fully. And everyone wants to prepare for the future.

Those are the same reasons that millions of people turn to diaries and journals.

Tarot cards and journals are magical tools that can help us spark our creativity. Both can help us develop our intuition and express our visions, hopes, and dreams. Both focus on the patterns of everyday experiences and one's place in a larger universe. Both are primarily instruments of the present moment, with a degree of reflection and prediction thrown in for good measure. Both can help us integrate our experiences and provide wide avenues for reflection, introspection, and self-development.

In fact, the issues that most people bring to a tarot reading are the same issues they bring to their journals: concerns about the past, qualms about the present, and questions about the future. They struggle with the desire to please themselves versus their need to please others. They hope for the future—and fear the unknown.

Ultimately, people who read tarot cards and people who keep journals are both participating in a creative process. They are engaged in acts of creation, of storytelling. They are actively weaving the fabric of their lives, spinning yarns, putting their own stories into context, and weaving together the past, present, and future. All told, they are on a quest for self-discovery.

The tarot is a natural partner in that quest. Tarot cards provide a ready-made framework for analysis and contemplation. The structure of the deck is holistic. The symbols on each card reflect the ancient myths and legends that shape our perceptions of the world, as well as the dramas of everyday existence. And because the tarot is firmly rooted in Western culture and tradition—including mythology, astrology, numerology, and the Bible—the cards are accessible to anyone familiar with modern life.

When you combine the use of the tarot with a journal, you create a powerful vehicle for growth and change. Adding tarot cards to a journaling routine can help you see yourself clearly, recognize obstacles, overcome barriers, express your concerns, and make the most of your gifts and talents. The tarot is an ideal tool for exploring your inner world, and the tarot journal is an ideal vehicle to house your record of your travels.

By incorporating tarot cards in your journal, you can have a pre-designed template for contemplating your existence. Through the cards, you can explore both the larger themes of the human experience and the variations of your everyday life.

If you come to this book as a journaler, I hope you will be inspired to find a deck of tarot cards and start adding them to your journaling practice. Even if you don't think of yourself as a tarot reader, the cards will help you bridge the communication gap between your conscious and unconscious minds, and provide a rich source of ideas and inspiration for your journals. The cards will guide you into extensive, deep, rich, and meaningful journeys—and more rewarding journaling.

If you come to this book as a tarot card reader, I hope you will be inspired to start a journal to complement your work with the cards. A tarot journal will help you personalize the cards, master the structure and symbolism of the deck, develop a rapport with the archetypes of the tarot, and access your intuition. By combining tarot and journaling, you can make the cards work better for you.

In either case, I have no doubt that you will immediately feel at home with the concepts and suggestions you are about to discover—and that you can create a tarot journal that will become a powerful tool for reflection, growth, and change.

Whether you want to access your higher self, discover ancient wisdom, or develop your intuition, a tarot journal will help you map your journey along both the inner and outer pathways of your existence.

Enjoy the trip—and don't forget to write!

Corrine Kenner

How to Use This Book

*J*n 1910, a metaphysician named Arthur Edward Waite published instructions for a tarot spread he called "An Ancient Celtic Method of Divination." It was an ingenious spread—quick, versatile, and so easy to use that even beginning tarot readers could get specific answers to their questions.

Since then, the Celtic Cross has become a perennial favorite among tarot readers. The spread is so popular, in fact, that most can even overlook one minor detail: Waite's "Ancient Celtic Method" isn't ancient, and it isn't Celtic, either. (In fact, Waite's secret society, the Order of the Golden Dawn, developed the spread for new members of the group just a few years before he introduced it to the general public.)

Nevertheless, for the last hundred years, the Celtic Cross has become a mainstay of tarot readers, who like the fact that they can use it to explore any subject or concern. Time after time, the Celtic Cross will offer a clear, concise overview of practically any situation.

The Celtic Cross

The Celtic Cross is an eleven-card spread. Each card represents a separate facet of a single issue. The first card, the significator, represents the subject of the reading. The second card illustrates the situation. The third card, which crosses the first two, describes any conflicts or opposing influences. Additional cards in the spread depict the foundation of the issue, the recent past, the highest ideals, the near future, self-image, public image, hopes and fears, and the most likely outcome of the current situation.

The Celtic Cross spread is easy to memorize. After you lay the significator at the center of the spread—because it is, of course, the central focus of the reading—you can use this mnemonic chant to help you remember where the rest of the cards go:

1. This covers you.
2. This crosses you.
3. This crowns you.
4. This grounds you.
5. This is behind you.
6. This is before you.
7. This is your self.
8. This is your house.
9. These are your hopes and fears.
10. This is what will come; this is the most likely outcome of your current path.

The card positions aren't arbitrary, and they didn't come about by coincidence. In fact, the Celtic Cross spread works so well because it is designed to reflect the way we think and the way we see the world.

Naturally, we all see the world from our own point of view—which seems, to each one of us, to be a central vantage point. We look back at our pasts and forward to our futures. We find a foothold in whatever foundation we have developed and we look up for guidance from our highest ideals. We picture ourselves in our own minds—and then we see other people reflect our words and

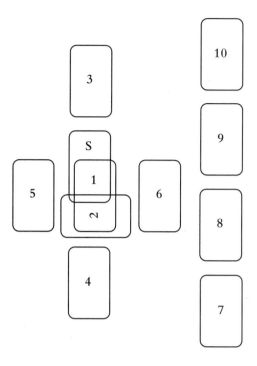

THE LAYOUT FOR THE CELTIC CROSS SPREAD.

actions back to us. Finally, before we dare to consider the most likely outcome of our current existence, we pause to contemplate our fondest hopes and our deepest, darkest fears.

In the years since its introduction, the Celtic Cross has served as the framework for countless tarot readings. The Celtic Cross also serves as the framework for this book. Each chapter of *Tarot Journaling* is based on the information the Celtic Cross spread is designed to impart. This book is an example of the fact that, like a journal, a written record can bring a tarot reading to life.

You don't need to know the ins and outs of the Celtic Cross to use this book. You don't need to be a master of the tarot or a long-time, experienced journaler. You just need a few basic supplies and a willingness to explore your life with the tarot as your guide.

If you are ready to start shuffling and let the cards fall where they may, gather your cards, your journal, and a pen, and you can get started.

The Basics: A Tarot Tutorial

While you don't need to be a tarot expert to use this book—or to create a tarot journal—your work will be easier if you understand the basic structure and symbolism of the tarot deck.

The tarot is a deck of seventy-eight cards divided into two sections: the Major Arcana and the Minor Arcana. The Minor Arcana has four suits. Each suit has ten numbered cards and four court cards, much like a standard deck of playing cards.

While that might seem like a lot to comprehend, it's actually an elegant design. Each component fits neatly inside the one that comes before it, like a set of Russian nesting dolls. Individually, each section of the deck seems complete in and of itself—until you open it and find there's another whole world tucked neatly inside.

What's more, the structure and the symbolism of the tarot deck is grounded in the real world. Because it reflects our shared experience as human beings, it's easier to understand than you might think.

The Major Arcana: Cosmic Forces

The Major Arcana, which is Latin for "greater secrets," is made up of twenty-two cards. The greater secrets are the big mysteries of life—like how we live, learn, fall in love, and find our true calling. For the most part, Major Arcana cards represent powerful cosmic forces that are usually outside our control.

The Major Arcana cards use a series of images to depict our journey through life, starting with the card of the Fool—a naive, innocent traveler about to embark on a journey of adventure and excitement. The Major Arcana cards also depict archetypal images that you will probably recognize immediately, such as the Lovers, the Hermit, Death, and the Devil.

Each one of those Major Arcana cards represents a universal concept, such as freedom, wisdom, patience, and optimism. Many of them also depict ancient gods and goddesses, who once served as role models for ordinary mortals. In today's more scientific parlance, each one of the Major Arcana cards represents an archetype.

Archetypes are universal expressions of the human condition. All cultures and civilizations, no matter where they sit in time or space, share similar archetypes—like the wandering fool, the powerful magician, and the mysterious, wise woman. Not coincidentally, those are the first three cards of the Major Arcana.

Each card of the Major Arcana depicts one stage in human development. All together, the Major Arcana cards combine to portray an allegorical view of our journey through life. The journey is sometimes called the Fool's journey, in honor of the Fool card who leads the parade. The rest of the Major Arcana consists of the Magician, the High Priestess, the Empress, the Emperor, the Hierophant, the Lovers, the Chariot, Strength, the Hermit, the Wheel of Fortune, Justice, the Hanged Man, Death, Temperance, the Devil, the Tower, the Star, the Moon, the Sun, Judgement, and the World.

The Major Arcana cards are usually easy to tell from the rest of the deck, because they are typically numbered with Roman numerals: I, II, III, and so on.

Set the Major Arcana cards aside and you will find that the second half of the tarot deck is equally fascinating. It consists of the fifty-six cards of the Minor Arcana.

The Everyday Cards of the Minor Arcana

The term *Minor Arcana* stands for the "lesser secrets" of the tarot. While the Major Arcana cards depict cosmic forces, Minor Arcana cards illustrate ordinary people and events. The Minor Arcana cards are no less important than their Major Arcana counterparts, but they do focus more on the activities of everyday life: going to work or taking time to play. Minor Arcana cards tend to depict average people doing commonplace things like dancing, napping, eating, and shopping.

The structure of the Minor Arcana will probably seem familiar to you if you have ever played card games like poker, rummy, or bridge. Just as a deck of playing cards is divided into the four suits of clubs, hearts, spades, and diamonds, the Minor Arcana is divided into the four suits of wands, cups, swords, and pentacles. Wands correspond to clubs; cups correspond to hearts; swords correspond to spades; and pentacles correspond to diamonds.

The Four Suits of the Minor Arcana

In tarot, each suit is more than just a way to divide the deck into manageable groups. In fact, each suit of the Minor Arcana is symbolic, because each one represents a separate realm of existence.

> *Wands.* The fiery suit of wands represents the realm of spiritual existence. Wands cards usually picture freshly cut branches from leafy trees, symbolic of the fire and burning passions of our spiritual life, our inspirations, and our primal drives—our quest for fire. Wands symbolize the fire and passion of spirit. One way to remember that is by picturing each wand as a flaming torch that can be used for light and heat—or, in other words, enlightenment and inspiration. (In some tarot decks, wands are called rods, batons, staves, or staffs.)

Cups. The watery suit of cups corresponds to the world of emotion. The cups cards, which usually depict drinking, toasting, and celebration, are centered on our relationships and commitments to other people. Cups, like their playing-card counterparts, the hearts, symbolize the richness and satisfaction of emotional life. Remember that cups hold water and wine—the essence of life—and cups can be used to toast our friends and family. (In some tarot decks, cups are called chalices.)

Swords. The airy suit of swords depicts the heady issues of thought and the intellect. The suit also symbolizes communication—because we can use words like weapons, both to defend our own ideas and to attack those with whom we disagree. (In some tarot decks, swords are called blades.)

Pentacles. The earthy pentacles cards symbolize the tangible realities of physical life. In the tarot, pentacles usually look like coins, and they represent the things we can touch, the things we can feel, and the things we treasure, both material and spiritual. (In some tarot decks, pentacles are called coins or discs.)

Numbered cards. There are ten numbered cards in each suit. Each card represents one step in a series of events, from beginning to end. Aces represent beginnings; tens represent conclusions.

Aces: new beginnings

2: duality and balance

3: blending and growth

4: solid foundations

5: upsetting the balance

6: re-establishing the balance

7: new awareness

8: re-evaluation

9: near completion

10: completion, prepare to begin again

Pages: lessons, news, messages

Knights: adventures, protection

Queens: safeguard, nurture

Kings: organization, defense

The Court Cards

The only structural difference between a deck of playing cards and the tarot's Minor Arcana is the addition of a few extra court cards. In addition to Jacks, which are called Knights in tarot, each suit of the Minor Arcana includes a King, Queen, and a Page. Occasionally, court cards carry other titles, such as Knave, Prince, and Princess. In most tarot decks, however, the four figures constitute a complete royal family: father, mother, son, and daughter.

Court cards have a wide range of functions. They can represent other people, or they can reflect aspects of your own personality. In a tarot reading, even cards that obviously refer to other people in your life actually relate to how you see yourself, and how you project your own likes, dislikes, and personality traits onto other people. For the most part, court cards tend to illustrate what you secretly think and feel about yourself, by helping you recognize and identify traits that you like and dislike in others.

Choosing a Tarot Deck

In order to keep a tarot journal and try the exercises in this guide, you will need a deck of tarot cards—ideally, a traditional tarot deck with seventy-eight cards.

The deck that serves as the de facto standard is Arthur Edward Waite's *Rider-Waite-Smith Tarot*. That's the same deck that Waite was writing about when he first introduced the Celtic Cross spread.

Waite designed the deck in 1909, and he hired artist Pamela Colman Smith to execute his designs. She took the groundbreaking step of adding a scenic illustration to every single card. Previously, only Major Arcana cards featured people and places; Minor Arcana cards generally consisted of a repeated motif, such as six cups in a row, or seven swords.

Pamela Colman Smith's innovation revolutionized the tarot. Suddenly, tarot card readers could interpret images, rather than memorize the meaning of each card or rely on their psychic impressions.

While the Rider-Waite-Smith deck is a perennial bestseller, it is not the only deck on the market. In fact, the Rider-Waite-Smith deck has engendered hundreds of derivative decks, such as the *Universal Tarot* and the *Gilded Tarot*—both good choices for use with this book. Other decks that lend themselves to use with a journal include James Wanless's *Voyager Tarot*, Anna Franklin and Paul Mason's *Sacred Circle Tarot*, and the *Robin Wood Tarot*.

If you are interested in myths, legends, classic stories, or the like, you might want to choose a specialty deck that reflects your interests, such as Anna-Marie Ferguson's *Legend: The Arthurian Tarot*, David Sexton's *Tarot of Oz*, or D. J. Conway and Lisa Hunt's *Celtic Dragon Tarot*. If you feel especially creative, you could even adapt the exercises in this guide to work with other types of divination decks, such as Anna Franklin and Paul Mason's *Fairy Ring Oracle* or Silver Ravenwolf and Nigel Jackson's *Witches Runes*. Ultimately, for the purposes of this book, you can use any tarot or tarot-style deck you like.

Actually, forget about finding a deck that you merely *like*. You will have the best results if you use a deck that you *love*.

The deck you choose should fascinate you. You should be mesmerized by the colors, the lines, the forms, and the style of each card. You should be attracted to the characters pictured in the cards. You should like their faces, their hairstyles, their body language, and their clothes. You should be inspired by their landscape and intrigued by their architecture. You should be able to recognize several of the artist's symbols—meaningful touches such as accessories, props, power animals, and astrological references. In fact, you should be able to imagine yourself living in that world—because on some level, you will be.

If you don't already own a deck of tarot cards, you can find one at most bookstores. When you go shopping for your deck, try to visit a store or a website that has a wide range of sample cards on display. Make sure that every card in the deck is fully illustrated; some decks, especially those that are reproductions of ancient historical decks, use a simple repeating pattern or motif for some cards, particularly in the Minor Arcana; those sorts of designs usually are not as inspiring as individual illustrations.

Look for art that appeals to you, in color, symbolism, and design. Examine the details of each image. Take time to shop around for an alternate reality that you really like. You're going to be spending a lot of time there.

Choosing Cards

For some of the suggestions in this book, you will work with one card at a time. For others, you will try your hand at simple card layouts and spreads. You can choose the cards you work with in several ways.

Follow the numbers. You could work your way sequentially through the deck. Start with the Fool, move on through the remaining twenty-one cards of the Major Arcana, and then work through the four suits of the Minor Arcana: wands, cups, swords, and pentacles.

Play favorites. Alternately, you could start with cards you especially like—or dislike. Start with all of the cards face up. Flip through them quickly. Set your favorites aside, and then narrow your choice down to the cards you need for the exercise.

Try your luck. On the other hand, you might like to take a ride on the Wheel of Fortune and let the deck choose a card for you. Clear your mind. Shuffle the deck and choose a card, either by cutting the cards or dealing the top card from the deck. Alternately, you could spread your deck face down across a tabletop and move your hand or dangle a pendulum over the cards until you feel drawn to the one you need.

No matter how you find your card—or your card finds you—don't worry that you might somehow get the "wrong" one. In tarot journaling, as in tarot reading, you will always get the card you were meant to see.

Order, Order!

When you read tarot cards, no one expects you to keep the deck in order. In fact, you are expected to shuffle the cards thoroughly, stirring and mixing and randomizing them until some are right-side up, some are upside down, and some have even been dropped on the floor.

When you read this book, you don't have to follow along in any particular order, either: you can work through the exercises in any sequence you like. You can start at page one and work your way through to the appendices and the blurb on the back cover. If you like, you can flip through the pages and pick an exercise at random—just as you can shuffle the deck and pick a card at random. You can start with the suggestions that interest you most, or you can choose an exercise based on a card that interests you.

Most of the activities in this guide can be used with any card in the traditional seventy-eight-card tarot deck. Most can be easily adapted to your specific needs. Some might even lead you to create your own activities for the cards—and truly make your tarot journal your own.

The Benefits of
Tarot Journaling

*J*ournaling will help you live a better life. Believe it or not, the simple act of keeping a journal has been scientifically proven to reduce stress, tension, anxiety, and depression—and researchers have shown that people who keep journals are better able to fight off opportunistic infections, so they get sick less often. A research psychologist at the University of Texas at Austin, James Pennebaker, found that regular journaling strengthens immune cells, called T lymphocytes. Joshua M. Smyth, Ph.D., associate professor of psychology at North Dakota State University, found that journaling decreases the symptoms of asthma and rheumatoid arthritis.

When you keep a tarot journal, your mind, body, and spirit will benefit. A tarot journal will help you sharpen your intuition, discover a new rapport with ancient symbols, and expand your worldview. As you become more familiar with the structure and symbolism of the tarot deck, you will connect more deeply with the archetypes of the tarot. Before long, you will see growth and progress, both in your tarot readings and in your everyday life.

The benefits of tarot journaling are countless, but you might think of them in general terms—as if they were laid out in the shape of the Celtic Cross.

Your self. A tarot journal is private, sacred space in which you can ruminate and ponder the big questions of your life and your existence. Your tarot journal will help you organize your thoughts and become a clearer, more logical thinker.

What covers you. Your tarot journal will help you understand the full scope of your present situation. A journal, like a tarot reading, is a study of current events and an instrument of the present moment. A journal is not an autobiography or a memoir —although you can use a journal to reminisce about your past. For the most part, a tarot journal will help you understand your present situation and experience your life more fully.

What crosses you. Journaling is an effective way to watch for roadblocks and spot obstacles in your path—including those that you put up yourself. You can use your tarot journal to deal with issues that perplex you or people who vex you. You can even use your tarot journal to explore and integrate your dark side. In the privacy of your journal's pages, you can acknowledge your own inherent badness—your hateful thoughts, hurtful wishes, and harmful desires. Like a willful, spoiled child, you can indulge your own antisocial self, rage against those who would control and subdue you, and lash out at situations that thwart your progress. Then you can find solutions.

Your foundation. The images and archetypes of the tarot don't merely exist on paper. They live in the realm of your conscious and unconscious mind, with the power to shape your attitudes, your beliefs, and your actions.

Your tarot journal will become the foundation for your work with the cards. Your own experiences with each card will personalize the tarot for you in ways you can hardly imagine. New insights and ideas about the cards will pop into your head, seemingly out of nowhere, and practically write themselves on the page.

The groundwork you lay in your journal will be the basis for developing your own interpretations of the cards—your personal symbol dictionary.

You can also use your tarot journal to spot correspondences and meaningful coincidences in your daily life. You can even use your tarot journal to record your dreams and free-form thoughts inspired by the cards, but not directly about the cards.

In short, your tarot journal can be a living record of how the tarot expresses itself in your daily life.

What crowns you. A tarot journal will help you tune in to your higher self and live up to your highest ideals. If your subconscious mind is trying to communicate with you, it can make contact on the pages of your journal. As you make notes about your world, you will probably start to notice more meaningful coincidences—more messages from the universe or a higher power. Ultimately, your tarot journal can help make you a more spiritual person.

Your past. Journaling is a widely recognized form of therapy. Your tarot journal will help you understand your past, release painful memories, and move on with your life. Your tarot journal will also help you tally your accomplishments and celebrate your successes. You can even use your tarot journal to explore alternate realities, to work through your regrets and missed opportunities, and, in some cases, literally rewrite history.

Your future. Your tarot journal can help you create the future you want. When you understand the connections between past and present events, you will be better equipped to predict the outcome of your current path, change course, and aim for the destination you truly want.

Your tarot journal will also help you manifest your destiny. When you write about your hopes and dreams, they become real. You give them shape and form and substance. You also prepare yourself, on some level, to accept the future you want.

Your self-image. Your tarot journal can improve your self-image and boost your self-esteem. Writing in your tarot journal will unblock your creative drives and prime the pump for a well-spring of related endeavors. You will be flooded with insights, inspirations, and creations.

Your tarot journal will also make you a better communicator. Just as reading books expands your vocabulary—painlessly and without conscious effort—the simple act of sitting down to write will help you hone your writing skills.

Your house. Your tarot journal will help you see yourself clearly—and see how others look at you. You can look at the world through a more objective lens, and you can use that information to help you heal rifts and develop happier, healthier relationships.

Your tarot journal can also help you become more interesting and attractive. You may find yourself taking more chances and being more active, just so you have something to write about in your journal—and talk about with other people.

In an interesting twist, your tarot journal can even help you feel less self-conscious. Writing about yourself can help you see yourself with less attachment and become more of an observer, with a broader view of your own life. Your tarot journal will help you see the big picture, so you won't need to take up a disproportionate space in the viewfinder.

Your hopes and fears. A tarot journal will help you articulate your hopes and face your fears. In your journal, you will have the absolute freedom to plumb the deepest depths and the highest heights of your existence, to explore the worst-case scenarios and "what if's," and to find solutions *before* you have problems.

Your most likely outcome. Your tarot journal will be a trusted ally and companion as you seek your fortune. You can use your tarot journal to envision your most likely future, and then you can change course if it seems that you are heading in the wrong direction.

Significant Decisions

HOW TO CHOOSE A
TAROT JOURNAL

> The Diviner first selects a card to represent the
> person or matter about which inquiry is made.
> This card is called the Significator. Should he wish
> to ascertain something in connexion with himself
> he takes the one which corresponds to his personal
> description.
>
> —ARTHUR EDWARD WAITE,
> *The Pictorial Key to the Tarot* (1910)

When tarot readers begin a session, they often choose
one card—the significator—to represent the subject of
the reading.

Choosing a significator is more of an art than a science. In most
cases, the significator looks like the person at the heart of the reading. You might pick the Queen of Wands for a fiery redhead, for
example, or use the Hierophant for a distinguished teacher. Sometimes, tarot readers choose a significator based on the question they
plan to ask or the intent of the reading. A man who is involved in a
lawsuit might choose Justice as a significator. The Empress card
would probably lend itself to use with a question about pregnancy.
In any case, the significator sets the tone, narrows the focus, and lays
the groundwork for the rest of the reading.

It's interesting to note that a tarot reader rarely deals the significator face down off the top of the deck, like other cards in a tarot spread. In fact, in almost every case, the reader chooses a significator by looking through the cards, face up, before the reading even begins. Once the significator is on the table, the rest of the cards can fall where they may.

Your Journal, Your Self

When you decide to keep a tarot journal, the type of journal you choose can be as important as the significator you select for a reading. Your journal, as Waite might say, should correspond to your personal description.

In other words, your journal should reflect your personality, because it will serve as a repository for your thoughts and feelings, and it will embody your wants, needs, and desires. If you are an executive, you might want a classic leatherbound journal. If you are an artist, you might need a sketchbook to hold all of your creative ideas.

Your journal should also suit your lifestyle, and it should be constructed in a way that will be physically comfortable for you to use.

The type of tarot journal you choose will help you focus your views, collect your thoughts, and clarify your emotions. It will help you relive your past, explore your present, and plan for your future. It will help you document your work with the cards and chart your growth. Ultimately, the type of tarot journal you choose will help you define yourself.

Choosing a Journal

I've kept a journal for years. Several journals, in fact.

I didn't say I've actually written in them. I've just kept them, on the shelf, because for one reason or another they didn't work out for me. Some were too big and heavy to carry around. Others were "too good" for my daily ramblings. Others I'm saving for something special. In the end, the journal I use most is an electronic journal, stored on my laptop's hard drive, with some sections posted on my blog, and others incorporated into books and articles.

You, too, may need to experiment until you find a journal that suits your needs.

If you choose, you can go looking for a journal, comparison shopping and visiting your favorite shops and stores. If you are more magically inclined, you can wait for your journal to find you; simply meditate and cast your intention out to the universe, so that you will be prepared to spot your journal when it crosses your path. In either case, the first step in selecting a journal is to think about the work you plan to do in it.

Types of Journals

There are many types of tarot journals. Some serve a single purpose, like a logbook. Others combine an eclectic mix of uses with a wide range of entries.

Diary. Your tarot journal might be a traditional, diary-style journal—a chronological log of daily or weekly events. In that case, your tarot deck will serve mostly as a tool for creative inspiration—a storehouse for reflections and ruminations about your everyday life, and a springboard to help you write about the events of your day, your impressions, and your insights.

Reading record. Your tarot journal might be a straightforward record of all of the tarot readings you have conducted. Most records would include the date, the questions you asked, and a diagram of the cards that turned up. You could even snap an instant photo or digital picture of your spread, and incorporate it into your journal.

If you are pressed for time during the reading, or if you uncover issues that you would like to explore later, you can refer to your tarot journal to re-create the spread for further analysis. If a reading confused you, your tarot journal can help you review it later, for further consideration and reflection. Then, as each situation unfolds, you can check your notes against the outcome.

The reading records you keep in your journal can be as simple or as elaborate as you like. Your records can even vary from reading to reading. For some sessions, you might jot just a few notes. For others, you might want to record every detail—especially the cards that seem most significant in the spread, important pairs and combinations, and any flashes of insight and intuition you might experience.

In the process, your record will also serve as an ersatz diary. As you look through your notes about each reading, you can remember where you were, whom you were with, the events that led up to the reading, and the events that were on your mind.

Card interpretation handbook. If you are a student of the tarot, someone has probably suggested that you make detailed notes about your own interpretations of every card in the deck. Your tarot journal is the place to start.

Some people begin by copying the information that comes with their decks, usually in the form of a little white booklet. You could include relevant quotes and commentary from other sources, such as books and web-based discussion groups. Before long, the information you get from other people will probably serve as a springboard for your own interpretations of each card.

Workbook. You might want to use your tarot journal in conjunction with a tarot workbook or home study course, such as
Mary K. Greer's *Tarot for Your Self,* Joan Bunning's *Learning the
Tarot,* Teresa Michelsen's *Complete Tarot Reader,* or Wald and
Ruth Ann Amberstone's *Tarot School Correspondence Course.* As
you follow the format each author presents, you can watch
your understanding unfold and flower on the page.

Simply use your tarot journal like a school notebook. Keep
a running record of each exercise and assignment, along with
the results you get when you try them. Also, keep related notes
about your thoughts, comments, and experiences as you complete each course of study.

Your tarot journal is also a good place to write your own
personal reviews of books you have read relating to the tarot,
or to make notes about tarot classes and thought-provoking
lectures and workshops you have attended.

Multi-disciplinary studies. You might like to develop a journal that
combines your tarot pursuits with related complementary
studies, such as astrology, numerology, runes, I Ching, Kabbalah, dream interpretation, tea-leaf reading, meditation, palmistry, or chakra balancing. Such esoteric pursuits usually dove-
tail surprisingly well with the tarot. In many cases, their
subject matter springs from the same metaphysical pool, and it
can be fascinating to spot the similarities and differences
between them.

By keeping a multi-disciplinary journal, you can learn more
quickly, become more flexible in your thinking, discover useful metaphors and analogies, and document and track your
overall development and growth.

Book of Shadows. When metaphysicians begin a formal study of the mystic arts and sciences, they often begin to compile a Book of Shadows—a secret book of magic, filled with hand-written records of spells, enchantments, rituals, and divination. Your tarot-based Book of Shadows might also include training techniques, guidelines, correspondences, and other supernatural materials.

Writer's notebook. If you are a poet, a short story writer, or a novelist, you might want to use your tarot journal as a writer's notebook. You can turn to the cards for inspiration and for insight.

Tarot cards can suggest characters, conflict, crisis, and resolution. Do you need to know more about your protagonist? Pull a card. Looking for a plot twist? Try a past, present, and future reading. Need an alternate point of view or a surprise ending? Shuffle the deck and let the cards fall where they may.

You can also use your tarot journal like a standard writer's notebook, and include snippets of dialogue, overheard remarks, observations, and story ideas to use in future writing projects. You could even use your tarot journal simply to record autobiographical stories about your life.

Special occasion journals. Nobody ever said a journal had to be perpetual. You could create a short-term tarot journal to mark birthdays, anniversaries, holidays, vacations, and other special events.

Artist's journal. Sometimes we talk about the cards so much that we forget that tarot is primarily a visual medium. In fact, Arthur Edward Waite himself referred to the tarot as a "pictorial" language. While most decks include titles and numbers on each card, words tend to be appended as an afterthought.

If you are creatively inclined—or even if you simply want to *feel* creative—you could begin an artist's journal and fill it with pencil, pen, and charcoal drawings, or paintings, or collage. Copy the images from your favorite deck. Draw scenes from your own life that remind you of the cards. Clip favorite photos from magazines and catalogs. Use your journal to hold images that remind you of the tarot or images you would like to interpret in light of the cards. Your artist's journal might even serve as the basis for a tarot deck of your own someday.

The Three P's

Keep these three things in mind as you choose your journal: portability, price, and permanence.

Portability. If you plan to carry your journal in a backpack or a purse, so you can write in coffee shops or on the train, you will probably want a lightweight, portable journal. On the other hand, if you tend to picture yourself writing in front of your fireplace with your dog curled at your feet, a heavy, leather-bound tome would be a natural choice.

Price. The price of your journal may be a factor in your choice—but price can be calculated as more than just the cost of a journal. Time is money, and your thoughts and words have value, too. If you are merely starting to experiment with journaling, you might use an inexpensive notebook. Be aware, however, that your tarot journal may soon become one of your most treasured possessions, and you might want to upgrade to a higher-quality book.

Permanence. If you use a bargain-basement journal, the paper will probably tear easily, turn yellow, and start to disintegrate within a few years. In fact, a cheap journal might not even last long enough to wear out; most just fall apart. If you want your journal to last for years, invest in a well-made book with archival-quality paper, and store it in a clean, dry area at normal room temperature. Even the best journals fare poorly if you lock them away in a freezing garage, a damp basement, or a hot, dry attic.

Form Follows Function

One of the characters in Michael Ondaatje's novel *The English Patient* kept an unconventional journal. He filled a volume of Herodotus' ancient Greek *Histories* with drawings, maps, and photographs. He wrote notes in the margins, and he tucked photographs and personal letters into its pages. In the process, he transformed the classic work into a memoir of his own.

Your journal can be as traditional or nontraditional as you like. Your journal might not even take the form of a book. You might outline your thoughts on the back of grocery store receipts. You might sketch your ideas on restaurant napkins, or scrawl notes on takeout menus.

You could also compose your thoughts on a yellow legal pad, collect your thoughts in a dime-store notebook, or write in a blank book from the stationery store. Or you could even travel to Italy or France and select a handcrafted, leather-covered diary.

Your perfect journal might take any of the following forms:

Three-ring binders. Three-ring binders make ideal tarot journals, because they are so versatile. You can add, delete, and rearrange pages as needed. You can use tabbed dividers to categorize your studies, and you can dedicate entire sections to Major Arcana cards, Minor Arcana cards, court cards, symbolism, history, mythology, or anything you like. You can add pocket pages to store magazine articles and news stories. You can print information you find on the Internet, punch your print-outs with a three-hole punch, and include them in your journal. You can even take just a few sheets of notepaper with you wherever you go, write whenever you like, and pop them into your binder when you get home.

Spiral notebooks. If you are just beginning to journal, and you are still experimenting with your own style of writing, a cheap starter journal will involve the least amount of risk—at least in terms of price—and you might feel freer to experiment with methods and style. A spiral notebook is a good place to start.

Spiral notebooks are available almost anywhere you shop. You can buy them at drug stores, grocery stores, discount stores, and gas stations. Spiral notebooks are cheap, easy to carry, and easy to store.

Unfortunately, spiral notebooks don't last long. The wire binding can bend and come loose, the pages can tear out, and the paper tends to turn yellow and start to decay within just a few years.

Composition books. Composition books—the notebooks with sturdy, speckled covers—make wonderful starter journals. Like other notebooks, composition books are inexpensive and readily available. The covers are usually stiff cardboard, which double as a firm writing surface. There is no wire binding to bend, work loose, or poke you as you work. Because the pages are sewn together, however, you can't tear out any pages or the whole book will fall apart. Composition books are generally not archival quality, so if you want to make them last you will need to use them gently and store them carefully.

Stenographer's notebooks. Like spiral notebooks, stenographer's notebooks are handy. Stenographer's notebooks are designed to be used on the run, and they are easy to work with if you plan to hold your journal on your lap as you write. They are sturdier than spiral notebooks—and a little classier, because they don't look like school notebooks. Stenographer's notebooks also are less conspicuous if you want to write privately in public places, and if you live with people who might be tempted to pry into a secret diary. However, stenographer's notebooks are not particularly durable, and they are not archival material. Treat them gently if you want them to last.

Memo pads and pocket notebooks. If you frequently write on the go or if you typically conduct tarot readings away from home, think about using a memo pad or pocket notebook for your journal. You can later transfer and expand upon your work in a larger, more permanent journal.

Blank books. Blank books come in a wide variety of prices, styles, sizes, and designs. Some feature lined pages, while others have blank pages. Some blank books have leather covers and ties, zippers, or snap closures. The best blank books are made of archival-quality paper and binding materials that will last for generations.

Refillable journals. Some journals are actually refillable; they consist of blank books that slide into attractive, long-lasting covers. Once you have filled one book, you can file the pages away and buy a refill for the cover.

Inspirational journals. Some blank journals are designed to inspire thoughts and ruminations, with stirring quotes and illustrations on each page. It may be interesting to note how a seemingly random quote or image can reflect the symbolism and the significance of the tarot card you write about.

Datebooks. While printed datebooks might remind you of the diary you kept in junior high—with five lines allowed for each day—today's datebooks can make great journals. Some datebooks feature a full page or two for every day of the year, and some include illustrations and inspirational quotes. If you hope to write every day, the format alone can be an incentive.

If you combine tarot with astrology, you might want to use an astrological datebook like Llewellyn's *Daily Planetary Guide*. By keeping your journal in an astrological calendar, you will automatically have a record of astrological phenomena, such as the positions of planets in signs, whenever you conduct a tarot reading or write in your journal.

Travel journals. In many ways, your travels into the tarot are like journeys into the inner world of your imagination. You might want to adapt a travel journal to use with your cards. A travel journal could help you document your adventures as though you were truly journeying to a new, exotic location—or rediscovering a land you once knew.

Artist's sketchpads. Lined paper serves as a guide to some writers. If you are a free spirit, however, you might not want to color inside the lines. Break the rules, and use an oversized artist's sketchbook for your journal. The format naturally lends itself not only to sketching, drawing, and painting, but also to creative writing. Unconstrained by arbitrary guidelines, your mind can wander on the page and your stream of consciousness can flow freely. You can even write sideways, at an angle, or in a spiral shape, for an artistic effect. Sketchpads are especially good for a type of entry called clustering, in which notes about one central thought or idea branch out in several directions.

Scrapbooks. You might want to go even further than an artist's sketchpad and use a scrapbook for your journal. The pages are huge, so you will have plenty of room to draw; construct timelines; paste photos, newspaper, and magazine clippings; and embellish your work with sketches, rubber stamps, sidebars, and follow-up notes and comments. You can even use a scrapbook to store found items that relate to the tarot: postcards, ticket stubs, letters, and other memorabilia.

Handmade journals. Many journal writers create their own handmade journals. There is a fine, subtle art to choosing—or making—the perfect paper, designing a cover, and binding one's handiwork. Handmade tarot journals can also be enhanced with unusual features such as pockets, sleeves, and mats to hold cards.

If you are interested in making your own tarot journal, look for a class in bookmaking or find instructions and supplies at a craft store.

Artist's portfolios. If your journal includes several unbound items, such as individual sheets of paper, flyers, brochures, newspaper tear sheets, magazine articles, Internet printouts, and sketches, you might want to store your collection in an artist's portfolio. Portfolios are custom-made folders with flaps that tie closed, designed specifically to hold and safeguard loose papers.

File folders. No one says that your journal needs to take the form of a book—especially if you tend to write on the go, on loose-leaf sheets of paper, on scratch pads, or on the backsides of envelopes. You might want to keep your entries in file folders, categorized by date or by subject. You can keep all of your files in a file drawer or an archive box designed to store documents and photos.

Index cards. Tarot card readers might be logically drawn to recording their observations on index cards, which are similar in size and shape to tarot cards themselves. What's more, a stack of blank three-by-five-inch cards can be a lot less intimidating than a series of blank pages. Index cards are an ideal way to free your creative mind and generate many ideas in a short amount of time—plus, you can fit a surprising amount of information on a single card. Start by dedicating one index card to each tarot card. As you branch out in your study of the tarot, use a new card for every thought that comes to mind. Through grouping the cards by subject, you will probably find that your ideas fall naturally into categories.

Electronic Journals

Some journalers insist that nothing can replace the feel of pen on paper. The physical act of writing, many believe, inspires creativity, stimulates the free flow of thoughts and ideas, triggers synaptic connections, and settles the nerves. The fact that handwriting has become something of a lost art form also lends charm to the concept of a handwritten journal.

On a practical level, however, electronic journals might prove to be a better option for some people.

For one thing, more people are comfortable with computers than ever before—and computers are accessible to everyone. Anyone who wants to log on can usually find a computer at home, at school, at work, or at a public terminal in a library or café.

As technology advances and becomes more affordable, an electronic journal can offer all of the benefits of a traditional journal, integrated with the convenience, portability, and accessibility of high-tech. Look for the following options:

Journaling software. You can use standard word-processing programs to keep a journal. You won't need to decipher poor handwriting, and you can cut and paste some selections for use in other projects. But for just a few dollars, you can also invest in software designed specifically for journaling. Like word-processing programs, journaling software usually includes a spell checker, thesaurus, and adjustable font and color schemes. Some packages will allow you to add digital images and sound files to your entries. Most journaling software also includes built-in prompts and quotations to inspire your writing, as well as automatic alarms for timed writing and automated help for devising lists and timelines.

Journaling software also makes it easy to keep multiple journals organized and cross-referenced by theme, topic, or subject. Your entries will be automatically archived and indexed, so you can search for entries by date, title, topic, or keyword. You can even encrypt your entries and protect them with passwords.

Remember, however, that technology is constantly evolving. The equipment and the programs you use today might not be available tomorrow. Even storage media will change. If you want to ensure that you will be able to read your journal in years to come, print it out periodically on archival-quality paper, just in case technology makes your computerized journal obsolete.

Blogs. Online journals—or web logs (blogs)—are open to anyone with access to the Internet and experiences to share. Some artists and writers, like *Gaian Tarot* creator Joanna Powell Colbert, use blogs to document the evolution of their projects.

For the most part, blogs are easy to create. Some online providers offer free blog hosting, while others charge about what you would pay for a website or Internet access. Entries appear chronologically, with automatic time and date stamps. Most blogs make it possible to post photos, sound files, and links to websites and related blogs.

Blogs are fun—but they aren't private, and they're not secure. Even if you only share your blog address with family and friends, anyone with web access can run a simple search and find your blog.

Blogs also can be transitory. If you plan to keep your entries forever, save them on your hard drive, archive them on storage media, and print them out on archival paper.

E-mail journals. While letter writing may be outdated, more people than ever are corresponding with each other via e-mail. E-mail is quick, comfortable, and familiar. If you already spend a portion of your day reading, writing, and checking e-mail, you might want to use it as the format of your tarot journal.

The process of writing e-mail and writing in a journal is very similar. In fact, a large number of journal entries are written in the form of a letter. Like journal entries, e-mail exchanges are written on the fly and in the present moment. Furthermore, most people write e-mails without a great deal of concern for perfect grammar, punctuation, and spelling—and most recipients don't expect award-winning prose, either. For the shy or self-conscious writer, e-mail can be ideal.

If you start an e-mail journal, you can share your entries with a trusted friend or family member. In that case, you will have an automatic copy of each message in your folder of sent items. You could also just mail your e-mail missives to yourself. You could even create a new e-mail identity and establish a separate account or folder for all of your journal entries. Each message will be filed chronologically, and you can search your e-mail journal by date, subject, message header, phrase, or keyword.

If you choose to keep an e-mail tarot journal, print it out periodically just to ensure that your entries won't be lost to a computer glitch or a server crash.

Audio and video recordings. Some people find it easier to start talking than to confront a blank page during the writing process. Others like to experiment with audio and video equipment. If you are a tech-minded person, an audio or video journal might be an ideal way to record your experiences with the cards. In fact, you might already have a head start on the process: many tarot readers are used to verbalizing their impressions of the cards and tape-recording their sessions with clients.

Today's technology makes it easier than ever to create top-quality recordings. As with all technology, however, bear in mind that storage and playback could become an issue. Equipment changes with time, players become obsolete and unavailable, and some media degrades with age. If you want your data to last, keep it stored in a dry, temperature-controlled area. Don't expose it to light, dust, dirt, or extremes of hot or cold. Also, be prepared to copy your files onto new standard mediums as they develop.

Multiple Partners

With so many attractive options available for your tarot journaling practice, you might be reassured to know that you don't have to choose just one. While you can consolidate many types of entries in a single journal, you might also decide you want to keep more than one journal.

You could keep one journal as a straightforward record of your readings. You might want to keep a pocket-size journal with your deck to record bare-bones notes about your readings. Later, you can expand on your thoughts about those readings in a second, larger journal.

If you use more than one tarot deck, you might want to keep a separate journal for each. You might also like to keep one journal for your study of the twenty-two Major Arcana cards and separate journals for each of the four suits. In that case, you could even color-code your journals: white or black for the Major Arcana, red for the fiery wands, blue for the watery cups, yellow for the airy swords, and green for the earthy pentacles. You might like to focus on a single card at a time, such as your birth card (see page 113 for one simple way to determine your birth card).

Ultimately, you can keep any type of journal or any number of journals you like. You can switch styles, change techniques, begin a new journal, or open a companion volume at any point. You are never under any obligation to finish a journal that's not working for you or tough it out with a technique that falls flat. Feel free to experiment, to play, and to have fun. A tarot journal is an excellent servant—but a bad master. Make sure your journal knows who's boss.

Get Personal

You can personalize your journal with a few simple techniques.

Cover. You can customize your tarot journal by decorating the cover with paint or collage. You can use images from the tarot itself or photos of people and places you like. You can use abstract or geometric designs. You might want to create a mandala—a circular design, like a stained glass window or a snowflake—that symbolizes spiritual wholeness.

Illuminate. You can illuminate your journal, like the medieval monks illuminated the books they copied in their scriptoriums. Even before you begin to write, you can draw or paint colorful borders on the pages of your journal. Then, as you compose individual entries, you can try sketching or drawing a few illustrations to accompany your writing. Later, you can color your artwork with markers or colored pencils.

Title. As you begin your new journal, consider giving it a title— but be sure you give your journal a title you can live with, because you could be laying the groundwork for a self-fulfilling prophecy. If you title your journal "The Troubles I've Known," the universe might think you're inviting more of the same—and you can probably expect to find yourself dealing with more trouble than ever before.

Later, you can also experiment with titling individual entries.

Epigraph. Open your journal with an inspirational quote or poem—an epigraph. Consider this one, from Josephine Hart: "There is an eternal landscape, a geography of the soul; we search for its outlines all our lives."

Table of contents. Leave the first few pages blank, so you can add a table of contents later. Number each page for future reference.

Dedication. Determine the theme of your journal, and make your intention for the journal clear. Then dedicate your journal to its mission or to someone you wish to honor with your work.

History in the making. Open your journal by telling the story of how you chose that particular journal and where you obtained it.

Accessorize Your Journal

In addition to choosing a journal, the right tools and accessories will help you focus your thoughts, unleash your creativity, communicate clearly, and work quickly and efficiently.

A tarot card altar. Create a portable tarot card altar by gluing an envelope, a plastic sleeve, or a ribbon to hold your tarot card of the day in your tarot journal. Or find a frame, a picture holder, or a clip to display a card in your journaling space. You might think of it as a tarot card altar.

Pens. If you are handwriting your journal, take time to find a pen that feels good in your hand and puts you in the mood to write. You might even want to use several pens, with different colors of ink for different types of entries.

Highlighters. You might want to use highlighters to mark especially important entries, keywords, and phrases, or to cross-reference your writing. You could color-code some entries, and use red highlights for fiery, spiritual, wands-style passages; blue for watery, emotional cups; yellow for airy, intellectual swords; and green for earthy, material, and physical pentacles.

Art supplies. Your journal doesn't have to be solely for writing. If you want to create a visual journal, you can use pencils, pens, markers, charcoal, watercolor, or acrylic paints.

A timer. If you plan to try timed writing for some of your entries, you will need a timer with an audible buzzer or bell. Any simple kitchen timer will work.

Storage bags. If you can sew, you might want to stitch matching bags for your journal and tarot deck, as well as a coordinating spread cloth to use when you work with the cards. Many tarot readers always lay their cards on a square piece of fabric, to keep them organized and clean. When the readings are over, they wrap their cards in the same cloth. Traditionally, tarot readers wrap their cards in black satin; you can use any fabric you like. Generally speaking, solid colors are best, because busy prints can distract from the images and symbols on your cards.

Storage basket or box. An attractive storage container will help keep your journal and your accessories at hand, so you can write whenever you feel the urge. Try a decorative basket or box.

1
What Covers You

> *Turn up the top or first card of the pack; cover
> the Significator with it, and say: This covers him.
> This card gives the influence which is affecting the
> person or matter of inquiry generally, the atmos-
> phere of it in which the other currents work.*
>
> —ARTHUR EDWARD WAITE,
> *The Pictorial Key to the Tarot* (1910)

Atmosphere and Influences

When Arthur Edward Waite first conceptualized his tarot deck, he
hired a young artist named Pamela Colman Smith to illustrate each
card. She was a fellow member of the Order of the Golden Dawn, a
mystical group that truly believed in the importance of atmosphere:
they met in a space designed to look like an ancient Egyptian pyra-
mid, and dressed in elaborate costumes with robes and headpieces.

Pamela Colman Smith had a theater background, so she fit right
in. Earlier, she had designed sets, costumes, and programs for Eng-
land's Royal Lyceum Theatre when it toured the United States—
and she brought her flair for the dramatic to the tarot cards she
painted. In fact, when you look through the Rider-Waite-Smith
deck, you might notice that many of the cards look like costumed
actors posing on a stage.

Your own backdrop and surroundings can play a crucial role in your journaling practice. If you want to get the most out of each performance, you might want to think about setting the stage and ushering in a little atmosphere.

Location, Location, Location

Where should you write in your tarot journal? You might like to work in a quiet room—especially if you plan to combine a full-fledged tarot reading with your writing, and privacy is an issue. In that case, a bedroom, a den, or a quiet corner in the yard is perfect. You might prefer to work where there is a buzz or hum of activity—where you can see the archetypes of the tarot come alive in the guise of busy strangers going about their business, and you can overhear stimulating snippets of conversation. Cafés, restaurants, coffee shops, libraries, and hotel lobbies are all good places to journal.

Honestly, you can write in your tarot journal anywhere you like, as long as you can immerse yourself fully in the tarot cards and in the pages of your journal—an area many tarot readers refer to as "sacred space."

Sacred Space

Many tarot readers routinely clear a sacred space for their tarot readings. The process is simple: they clear away clutter and distractions, light candles, and visualize pure white light filling their reading area.

Some tarot readers go a step further and establish a dedicated reading area. Many tarot readers like to enhance that sacred space with symbolic representations of the four suits and their corresponding elements, such as candles for fire, chalices for water, soothing background music for air, and crystals for earth.

In a similar fashion, tarot journaling should incorporate the four realms of your experience: spiritual, emotional, intellectual, and physical. Tarot journaling should also be a holistic experience that integrates all of your senses: sight, hearing, smell, taste, and touch.

The imagery and colors of the cards, of course, will please your sense of sight. Beautiful background music will uplift your spirit. Scented oils, candles, or incense will stimulate your sense of smell. A glass of water, coffee, tea, or wine will appeal to your sense of taste. And the weight of your journal in your hands or on your lap will put you in physical contact with your sense of touch.

Because the work you do in your tarot journal originates in your mind, however, you have one option that isn't open to you when you conduct a tarot reading. When you write in your tarot journal, you can work with sacred space that's based more in your inner world than in your outer reality. You might think of it as "imaginary" sacred space—except for the fact that it will seem more real to you every time you visit.

You might choose a scene from a tarot card as the basis for your sacred space. You might envision yourself in the Nine of Pentacles garden, for example, or the seaside balcony in the Two of Wands. You can either select a card at random or choose the card you most want to use.

Your sacred space also can be an idealized space that you picture in your mind's eye: the den, library, tea parlor, or landscape of your dreams. You might even find a photo in a magazine and use that as inspiration.

Imaginary sacred space is ideal for journaling, because it can travel with you. Imaginary sacred space is always ready for you to close your eyes and step inside—and cleanup is quick and easy. In addition, fantasy sacred space has the added benefit of preparing you to someday discover or create your ideal sacred space in the real world.

Ritual and Routine

Tarot reading rituals help smooth the way for tarot readings, by eliminating decisions about where you should sit, how you should shuffle, or how you should open a reading. Likewise, a few well-designed journaling rituals will help you get the preliminaries out of the way, calm you, and free you to start the creative process of writing.

Here are some techniques you can try as part of your journaling routine.

Light a candle. Gaze into the flame for a few minutes before you begin writing.

Enjoy your favorite drink. Feel yourself relax with every sip, and imagine it filling you with energy.

Try four-part breathing. Inhale, and hold your breath for five seconds. Then exhale, and again hold your breath for five seconds. As you breathe, imagine yourself becoming more relaxed and, simultaneously, more rejuvenated. Let the fresh air permeate every cell of your being. Inhale to recharge. Exhale to dispel tension and negativity.

Progressive relaxation. Consciously relax every part of your body, from head to toe.

Ground yourself. Put both feet on the floor. Imagine that you are a tree, with roots reaching far underground and branches reaching toward the heavens.

Starting Points

You might want to begin each entry the same way, so you don't waste any time composing your first few words.

Greet your audience. "Dear Diary" is cliché, but it works. You might also address each entry directly to the audience you have in mind. You might be writing your journal for your current self or your future self. You might imagine yourself writing to your children, your grandchildren, your students, your therapist, or your support group. You might be talking to your partner—past, present, or future. You might be writing to a friend—either someone you know now, someone you used to know, or someone you hope to meet.

Date the page. Include the time of day and your location.

Mood lighting. Write about your mood and the reason for your attitude. Recap the events of your day so far.

Draw a card. Choose a card from your tarot deck, and write its title on the page.

Shortcuts and Abbreviations

In tarot journaling, you might find yourself writing many of the same phrases, words, and titles over and over again. You can take shortcuts, like the abbreviations and shorthand that follow. If you choose to develop your own tarot timesavers, create a key and keep it with your journal.

Major Arcana Abbreviations

You can refer to Major Arcana cards by their Arabic numbers or Roman numerals, both of which are usually printed on the cards, and both of which are fairly standard and consistent from deck to deck. The only exception is Strength and Justice—cards 8 and 11. In some decks, depending on the artist's preference, Strength is 8 and Justice is 11. In other decks, that's reversed. In your journal, you might need to note which deck you're using.

ARABIC NUMBER	ROMAN NUMERAL	MAJOR ARCANA CARD
0	0	The Fool
1	I	The Magician
2	II	The High Priestess
3	III	The Empress
4	IV	The Emperor
5	V	The Hierophant
6	VI	The Lovers
7	VII	The Chariot
8	VIII	Strength (sometimes Justice)
9	IX	The Hermit
10	X	The Wheel of Fortune
11	XI	Justice (sometimes Strength)
12	XII	The Hanged Man
13	XIII	Death
14	XIV	Temperance
15	XV	The Devil
16	XVI	The Tower
17	XVII	The Star
18	XVIII	The Moon
19	XIX	The Sun
20	XX	Judgement
21	XXI	The World

Minor Arcana Abbreviations

You can use abbreviations for cards in the four suits of the Minor Arcana: typically W for wands, C for cups, S for swords, and P for pentacles. If your wands are called rods, use an R. If your wands are called staffs, distinguish them from swords by writing "St" and "Sw." If pentacles happen to be called coins in your deck, use a "cents" symbol (¢) instead of the letter C. You get the idea.

When you abbreviate the names of court cards, be sure to distinguish between Knights and Kings by using the abbreviations Kn for Knights and K for Kings.

	WANDS	CUPS	SWORDS	PENTACLES
Ace	AW	AC	AS	AP
Two	2W	2C	2S	2P
Three	3W	3C	3S	3P
Four	4W	4C	4S	4P
Five	5W	5C	5S	5P
Six	6W	6C	6S	6P
Seven	7W	7C	7S	7P
Eight	8W	8C	8S	8P
Nine	9W	9C	9S	9P
Ten	10W	10C	10S	10P
Page	PW	PC	PS	PP
Knight	KnW	KnC	KnS	KnP
Queen	QW	QC	QS	QP
King	KW	KC	KS	KP

If you prefer, you can also devise glyphs or symbolic illustrations to designate specific cards. You might note your wands as straight lines (|) or exclamation marks (!), cups as circles (o), swords as arrows (↑), and pentacles as stars or asterisks (*). You could even rely on playing-card symbols, and denote wands as clubs (♣), cups as hearts (♥), swords as spades (♠), and pentacles as diamonds (♦).

Reversed Cards

Many tarot readers note reversed cards with the ℞ symbol—a shortcut borrowed from astrologers, who use it to refer to retrograde planets. (Those are planets that appear, from Earth's vantage point, to be moving backward.)

Astrological glyphs can be useful additions to a tarot journal. Astrological references are built in to most tarot cards. The glyphs are not difficult to memorize, especially once you realize that they actually look like the symbol they represent.

Astrological Glyphs

GLYPH	SIGN. (REPRESENTATION.) CARD.
♈	Aries, the ram. (A ram's horns.) The Emperor.
♉	Taurus, the bull. (A bull's head.) The Hierophant.
♊	Gemini, the twins. (Twins, side by side.) The Lovers.
♋	Cancer, the crab. (A crab's claws.) The Chariot.
♌	Leo, the lion. (A lion's mane.) Strength.
♍	Virgo, the virgin. (MV, the Virgin Mary's initials.) The Hermit.
♎	Libra, the scales. (Balanced scales.) Justice.
♏	Scorpio, the scorpion. (A scorpion's stinger.) Death.
♐	Sagittarius, the archer. (An arrow.) Temperance.
♑	Capricorn, the goat. (A mountain goat.) The Devil.
♒	Aquarius, the water-bearer. (Waves of water or air.) The Star.
♓	Pisces, the fish. (Two fish, kissing.) The Moon.
☉	The Sun, luminary of light and illumination. (The center of the universe.) The Sun.
☽	The Moon, luminary of reflection and receptivity. (A crescent moon.) The High Priestess.
☿	Mercury, planet of speed and communication. (A magician in a horned headpiece.) The Magician.

♀   Venus, planet of love and beauty. (A woman's hand mirror.) The Empress.

♂   Mars, planet of energy and force. (Directed energy, an arrow.) The Tower.

♃   Jupiter, planet of luck and expansion. (The fourth planet from the Sun, the number four.) The Wheel of Fortune.

♄   Saturn, planet of boundaries, tradition, and limitations. (A traditional church with a steeple and cross.) The World.

♅   Uranus, planet of rebellion and independence. (A man doing a handstand.) The Fool.

♆   Neptune, planet of glamour and illusion. (The sea god's trident.) The Hanged Man.

♇   Pluto, planet of unavoidable change and regeneration. (A *P* and an *L*, the first two letters of "Pluto.") Judgement.

Checklists

You can save time during a journaling session by using a checklist to record pertinent facts about your tarot readings. The following list of possible checklist entries is extensive; don't try to incorporate all of it. Just pick and choose from the items on this list that truly interest you.

Some of the items you might want to include in your reading records include:

- The date
- The time
- Your location
- Astrological data (Sun sign, Moon phase, planetary retrogrades, void-of-course Moon data)
- The reader's name, if you are getting a reading from a friend
- The querent or questioner's name, if you are reading the card for another person

- The question or concern
- The name of the deck
- The name of the spread
- The cards in each position of the spread
- Encouraging cards
- Discouraging cards
- Surprising cards
- Clarification or wild cards
- Number of Major Arcana cards
- Number of Minor Arcana cards
- Significant details
- Keywords and phrases
- Numerical significance and interpretation
- Interesting pairs and combinations
- Predominant suits and elements
- Predominant colors
- Missing suits and elements
- Positive interpretations
- Negative connotations
- Intuitive response
- Spiritual response
- Emotional response
- Intellectual response
- Physical response
- Themes (elemental, numerical, astrological, or kabbalistic)
- Hebrew letter
- Kabbalistic sephiroth
- Kabbalistic pillar

- Color scale
- Additional questions developed during the course of the reading
- Insights
- Conclusion(s)

Fill in the Blanks

If you truly want to keep a quick and easy tarot journal, you might want to develop standard "fill in the blank" pages to document most of your readings. You can use any page design software to create forms like the ones in appendix V, print as many copies as you need, and keep them in a three-ring binder. You can also find download-able versions of each page online at www.tarotjournaling.com.

2

What Crosses You

Turn up the second card and lay it across the first, saying: This crosses him. It shews the nature of the obstacles in the matter. If it is a favorable card, the opposing forces will not be serious, or it may indicate that something good in itself will not be productive of good in the particular connexion.

—ARTHUR EDWARD WAITE,
The Pictorial Key to the Tarot (1910)

Journaling Obstacles and Stumbling Blocks

Tarot cards don't pull many punches—and the Celtic Cross is one of the most direct tarot card spreads you will ever find. It's not for the dainty or the faint of heart. It doesn't pussyfoot around, or hint at obstacles or problems. It doesn't even ask if you want the good news or the bad news first. It simply lays everything on the table and lets you make of it what you will.

The crossing card in the Celtic Cross depicts obstacles and stumbling blocks. In that vein, if you are starting a tarot journal, you may as well know what difficulties you might face. Happily, most of them are fairly common, and most have simple solutions.

Fear of Commitment

Few people can pick up a notebook and start keeping a journal. Journaling is a habit, and habits take time to establish. Journaling also takes commitment—and that can feel like hard work. If you start to delve too quickly into powerful emotions, painful memories, or liberate your creative process and generate too many ideas, your psyche may react, resist, feel overwhelmed, and want to stop.

Try a one-night stand. If you dread the thought of adding to your list of obligations, commit only for the short term. Plan to keep a journal for just an hour, an evening, or a weekend. If you like the experience, you can start another journal to use more often—or just plan to keep other short-term journals whenever you have time.

Make it a quickie. Set a timer and write for five minutes. Don't worry about scheduling your session or setting up a sacred space or following any pre-set format. Simply agree to sit down and write for five minutes at a time.

The buddy system. Ask a friend to keep a journal, too. You can meet for short journaling sessions, share selected passages, and encourage each other to keep writing.

Reward yourself. Plan to treat yourself to something after each journaling session. You might reward yourself with a new pen, for example, or a cup of coffee, or a nap.

Writer's Block

When it comes down to writing time, the blank page can be intimidating. When you keep a tarot journal, however, you never have to fear writer's block. Inspiration is as close as your favorite tarot deck.

Describe it. You can start by pulling a card at random and describing it in your journal. Then determine how the card you have pulled from the deck relates to your current situation. In effect, use your journal to conduct a one-card reading for yourself.

Draw a card. Literally, draw a card. Copy the card, or choose one object or image from the card and draw it in your journal. Then write about what that object means to you, how you felt as you drew it, and why you chose to draw it. See where it leads, and follow along in your journal.

Just do a reading. Conduct a full-fledged tarot reading for yourself and document your results.

Be here now. Write about where you are now, in the present moment. Note any insights and inspirations the tarot might have for your situation.

Performance Anxiety

You might be worried about what others would think of you if they found your tarot journal. Don't. You should be writing your journal only for yourself.

You might also be worried about living up to the high expectations you have for yourself. That's a tougher obstacle to overcome—but it can be done.

Loosen up. Any Empress can tell you that giving birth to your creative self can be a messy process. Don't worry about keeping your journal particularly neat or making it into a work of art—although you may lay the groundwork there for a creative masterpiece. Think of your journal as a rough draft. Don't edit or rewrite your entries. Don't cross out words, second-guess your spelling, or feel self-conscious about your storytelling ability.

Give yourself the freedom to make mistakes—and the freedom to make a mess.

Perfectionist tendencies. Don't worry about spelling, grammar, style, punctuation, or structure. Just write like you talk. You will automatically find your own voice, your own style, and your own fluid way of writing. Believe it or not, the less you worry about your writing, the better your writing will be.

Focus on quantity, not quality. Your journal is a rough draft of your experiences and your impressions. Rather than trying to make each entry an award-winning essay, plan only to write a certain number of words or a certain number of pages. "Don't get it right," James Thurber advised. "Just get it written."

Be playful. Tarot cards were first invented as a game. Your work with them should be playful, not laborious. If you find yourself getting too serious, and it's dragging you down, look for a lighter topic to write about in your journal.

Motive. Remember that you keep a journal because you want to, not because you have to. Don't be obsessive or compulsive. If you really don't want to write, put your journal away for a while and try again later.

Time Management

No matter how busy you are, you can find a way to fit journaling into your schedule.

Get into the habit. Try writing at the same time and in the same place every day, until journaling becomes a habit. Most people seem to have the most success by writing first thing in the morning or just before bed.

Make a standing appointment. Try to write at the same time every day, for the same amount of time. Take a cue from Peter De Vries, who said, "I write when I'm inspired, and I see to it that I'm inspired at nine o'clock every morning."

Stolen moments. Carry a tarot card and a small notebook in your pocket or purse, and journal whenever you have a spare moment.

Set goals. You might want to try daily entries, weekly entries, or some other regular schedule, such as three times a week. Remember to set aside special journaling sessions on holidays, anniversaries, and other special, meaningful dates. Also, set goals for the time you will write at each sitting: you might want to promise yourself just five minutes at a time, or fifteen minutes, or thirty minutes. Set a timer and follow through.

Procrastination

Procrastination is one of the seven deadly sins for anyone who wants to write.

Granted, before you start to work in your journal, you *should* be mentally prepared. You *should* be physically comfortable. You *should* have all of the supplies you need, set up ahead of time and positioned at the ready. You *should* be free of any distractions that could interfere with your train of thought.

And most of us should be so lucky. Unfortunately, there will always be dirty dishes in the sink, or a phone call that needs to be returned, or a light bulb that needs changing somewhere in your house.

Those things can wait.

You could also spend time cleaning your journaling area and organizing your journaling supplies.

Don't do it.

The only way to stop procrastinating is to sit down in a chair and start writing.

If you absolutely can't seem to get started, set a kitchen timer for just five minutes or ten minutes or fifteen minutes—whatever length of time seems minimal and painless. Once you get started, you will probably want to keep going.

Bad Cards

Tarot journals are, of course, firmly grounded in your experiences with tarot cards. You might encounter those cards during the course of a routine tarot reading. You might choose cards to write about by shuffling and dealing from the top of the deck. You might cut the cards or pull one at random. You might even find a card because it works its way loose from the rest of the deck and falls onto the floor.

But what if you sit down to write in your journal, only to find that you're working with the "wrong" card?

Never mind how you got the card. You just know it's wrong. It looks ugly, it gives you the creeps, it's got nothing to do with how you feel or what you did yesterday or what you plan to do today. It's completely out of place. It's irrelevant. It's insulting.

In that case, write about that. Write about how much you hate the card. Write about how you don't understand the card. Write about how you must have shuffled incorrectly, or somebody came in and messed with your cards when you weren't looking, or the universe is mocking your best efforts to keep a tarot journal and get a little insight into your life, and it's all terribly unfair.

Complete this sentence: *This card is the wrong card for me because*

——————————————.

Then sit back and realize that you can't really get the "wrong" card. In journaling, as in tarot reading, you will always get the card you were meant to see. When you keep a tarot journal, you will find inspiration in any card you pull from the deck, even if you are surprised by what the card reveals.

When the card that turns up seems wildly inappropriate, look for the reason you received it. Did you recognize the figure in the card as some aspect of yourself or someone you know? Is it a joke, merely exaggerating some point that you've been taking too seriously? If you really can't tell, try some of the writing prompts at the back of this book.

If all else fails, you can always have the upper hand. You don't have to play the cards you are dealt. You don't have to suffer at the fickle hand of fate. You are in charge of your destiny, and you can write about any card you want. If you are absolutely convinced that you have pulled the wrong card, put it back in the deck and choose another.

Negativity

Sometimes, you might find yourself turning to your journal only when you feel angry, unhappy, or disappointed. A journal is an ideal place to unload all of your negative emotions. If you like to think of yourself as a happy, positive person, however, it can be a shock to re-read your journal entries and find that they all seem to paint a distorted picture of yourself.

If you find yourself spending more time on the dark side than you would like, you can take steps to ensure that your journal entries remain balanced—and that you maintain your reputation as a happy medium.

Embrace your dual nature. In the world of the tarot, ideas, concepts, and themes are consistently depicted in pairs: male and female, light and dark, day and night, summer and winter, hot and cold, birth and death, yin and yang. The twofold nature of the tarot helps us see both sides of any issue—and you can use the imagery of the cards to see both sides of any situation. Look for cards that seem to illustrate your situation. Take note of the positives that are associated with that card, as well as the negatives.

Pros and cons. Make lists of all the pros and cons that apply to your situation.

Go to extremes. In some cases, it can be highly informative to be as negative as possible. Think of the Devil card: most illustrations depict the most extreme version possible, with horns and cloven hooves, a malefic grin, and a couple paralyzed by their own fears. If you're going to be negative, then by all means, be negative. Go all out, and write the most negative entries you can conceive of. Binge on your own misery—and then purge, so you get it all out of your system.

Meanwhile, back at the ranch . . . After you have completed a particularly negative entry in your tarot journal, you can append it to describe the other events you are dealing with in your life. Whether they are glowingly positive or merely routine, they will help balance your review.

Spin doctor. Rewrite your negative entries in the most positive light possible, as though you were conducting a public relations campaign on your own behalf.

Praise yourself. Journaling is a rewarding way to recognize, praise, and compliment your good qualities, and offer positive self-talk. Too many of us spend more time berating ourselves for mistakes, errors, fumbles, and faux pas than we do congratulating ourselves for the things we manage to do right. Did you turn in your weekly report on time? Did you remember to feed the cat? Did you help an old woman across the street? Congratulations! You can use your journal to compliment yourself and revel in your successes.

Be true to your school. Tarot readers have certain ethical responsibilities when they read cards for other people. As a tarot reader keeping a tarot journal, you also have a similar ethical responsibility toward yourself. Just as you would never use the cards to predict gloom and doom for another person, don't use tarot cards to beat up on yourself. Be as respectful, objective, open, honest, and optimistic when you work for yourself as you would for someone else.

Critical Opinions

If you have ever tried to write anything—including a journal—you have probably met your inner critic. You might not have been formally introduced, but he's the hissing little demon that stands behind you, always just out of sight, looking over your shoulder as you write. It's his voice that tries to stop you from writing, tries to get you to change what you write, and tries to make you question and doubt your own experiences.

You can evade your inner critic—and you can even outsmart him.

Take dictation. Write down whatever your inner critic says. Put it in your journal, in black and white. In the bright light of day, you can see how ridiculous your critic is—and cast him aside.

What a bunch of crap. You're an idiot. Your writing doesn't even make sense. You're crazy. You need a doctor. If anyone ever read this stuff, they would know for sure how stupid you are.

That's pretty easy to disregard, isn't it?

Write for someone specific. Imagine that you are writing your journal for a friend, a family member, or your future self. Tell your inner critic that he is not the intended audience, so his comments are not germane.

Write back to your critic. Answer his criticisms. Tell him where he's wrong—and tell him when he's right. Give the devil his due. After all, most critics just want someone to agree with them.

> *You're right. I can be an idiot. I don't always know what I'm doing—especially when I first sit down with only a glimmer of an idea. That's what this journal is for. I'm sorting out my thoughts, putting pen to paper, and attempting to make sense out of all my ideas. You are more than welcome to take part. Just let me know where you think I'm wrong, and tell me how you think I can fix it.*

Keep writing. Don't think you can win by losing. Your inner critic won't know what to do with himself if you quit writing and take his job away. He'll just criticize you for stopping and start harping at you to get back to the journal.

Meet your critic. Ask your critic for a formal introduction. Ask your critic for his name, his life story, his likes and dislikes. See if you have anything in common.

Find your critic in the cards. Choose a tarot card to represent your inner critic. If you choose the card on purpose, he might look like the Devil or the duplicitous Five of Swords or the glowering King of Swords. You might also choose a card at random. Consider the possibilities. What if your inner critic is the beatific Empress? Is she hiding a dark side? What might that say about you?

Dialogue with your critic. Question, interview, and challenge your critic.

Q: *Why are you bothering me?*
A: *I'm not trying to bother you. I'm just trying to be helpful.*

Q: *How are you being helpful?*
A: *I'm preparing you for the comments that other people are going to make.*

Q: *I'm not planning to show this to anyone else.*
A: *Are you sure?*

Q: *Positive. I'll call you if I need you to review anything I write for others, okay?*
A: *Okay. Just promise you'll call, all right? That's what I'm here for.*

Negotiate with your critic. Offer a compromise.

If you leave me alone for fifteen minutes, you can add your comments afterward.

Find an advocate in the cards. Now choose a tarot card to represent your advocate, your cheering section. Let your advocate duke it out with your inner critic. Imagine, for example, that you have chosen the King of Swords as your advocate.

King of Swords: You have overstepped your bounds.
Devil: I have no bounds.
King of Swords: This sword in my hands says otherwise. Back off!

Let others do the work. Determine which card represents your inner writer, struggling to achieve and accomplish. Then decide which card represents your most vocal, most troubling, most annoying judge, jury, and executioner. Replace that foe with an inner fan, an inner supporter, and if necessary, an inner editor who will come out for a gentle, supportive rewrite. Who plays which role could very well change from day to day. Just watch the interaction and record the results in your journal.

Work faster than your critic. While journaling is a reflective process, it should be anything but slow and leisurely. The best, most productive journal work is done quickly. Just write. Get your impressions out of your head and onto the page. Give your subconscious mind the freedom to express itself without hesitation, without second-guessing, without criticism. You can analyze it later. And you will probably surprise both yourself and your inner critic.

Stay in bed. For many of us, the bed is the consummate sacred space. We are born in bed, we die in bed, we create new life in bed, and we share our most intimate selves in bed. We reinvigorate ourselves, reinvent ourselves, and dream in bed. When we seek comfort, healing, solace, or retreat, we go to bed.

What's more, we rarely do anything particularly difficult or taxing in bed. Try writing there, either as you are about to fall asleep or just as you wake up. If you look as though you are just lying around, your inner critic might not be tempted to crawl underneath the covers and annoy you.

Write on index cards. Nobody could realistically believe that the comments you scrawl on index cards could ever be mistaken for serious writing. To criticize your notes would be as pathetic as criticizing your grocery list.

Remember that you were born to write. Writing comes as naturally as breathing. We are all born with an innate ability to use words, to label objects, and to master our environment with language. We all want to describe our emotions and to share our insights and observations with other people. We all want to communicate, and we all want to leave our mark. Just as prehistoric people inscribed their stories on the walls of caves, we all want to leave a record of our thoughts, our ideas, and our experiences. Don't let your inner critic take that away from you.

Get Guidance

Just as you can find your critic and an ally in the cards, you can also find a guide—a figurative escort and companion into the mysterious world of the tarot. You might even want to think of your guide as a literal tour guide—one who can lead you in and out of the cards, introduce you to friendly locals, show you the most scenic vistas, and shepherd you safely through shortcuts and down the occasional dark alley.

You can choose your guide from the cards consciously, simply by selecting any character from the tarot deck. Alternately, you might find that your guide seems to choose you, either by showing up repeatedly in your tarot readings, walking into one of your meditations, or popping up unexpectedly in your dreams.

You can work with any card to which you feel drawn. You can find your guide at random by shuffling and dealing a card face down. Or you can use a pendulum, dangling it over a fanned-out deck and letting it indicate the card you should select.

You can even work with a series of guides—some short-term, some long—by working your way systematically through the Major Arcana or through the entire seventy-eight-card deck.

You can get to know your guide better through meditation, dialogues, free or timed writing, and some of the other journaling techniques in this book. You can meet with your guide before you begin a routine reading or journaling session, or you could schedule recurring sessions with the same guide card, just as if you were meeting with a counselor in the real world. You can ask your guide for help in interpreting a single card or an entire layout, or you can ask your guide to help you focus on a question for the cards. Once you have chosen your guide's card, pull it from the deck and set it aside so you can refer to it during a reading or journaling session.

If you plan to do long-term work with a single guide, do some research into his or her background. Learn whether or not your guide has made historical appearances in myth or legend, in the guise of a god, goddess, or hero. The Empress, for example, is often compared to Demeter, the Greek goddess of the harvest and the mother of the lost Persephone, while the Hermit is sometimes thought to be Merlin the magician. Any book or encyclopedia of mythology can give you ideas, or you can learn more about tarot card associations through specialized tarot decks like the *Mythic Tarot* by Liz Greene and Juliet Sharman-Burke, or *Legend: The Arthurian Tarot* by Anna-Marie Ferguson.

Some cards are also associated with real-life historical figures: the Hanged Man, for example, could sometimes represent Judas or Mussolini. The Emperor could be Caesar or Napoleon. Keep your own knowledge of ancient and modern history in mind when you refer to the cards.

Once you know something of your guide's background, look for contemporary allusions to him or her in popular books, movies, or television shows. The *Star Wars* series, for example, is filled with archetypal characters who have tarot-card counterparts.

Also look for common interests and experiences that you share with your guide.

You might even want to research the etymology of your guide's name: you could discover that you share a name, or a variation of your name, with a character in the cards.

Twenty-Two Tips for Tired Journals

Sometimes, you might not seem to be facing any major obstacles in your journaling practice . . . but your work will just seem a little dull or a little dry. Here are twenty-two tips for reviving a tired journal.

1: Augment your journal. Go back through your previous journal entries. Highlight the interesting passages. Elaborate and expand upon your earlier notes.

2: Footnote your work. Add footnotes, explanatory comments, and conclusions to your journal entries.

3: Read your journal almost as you would read tarot cards. Look for words, phrases, and entries with deeper symbolic meaning than you ascribed to them as you wrote them. Look for messages.

4: Create. Turn one of your journal entries into a story, a song, a poem, a drawing, or a painting.

5: Consult a guidebook. If you can't find a direction you like, turn your journal into a directed study. There are many tarot handbooks and workbooks on the market. Find one you like, and enjoy the structure it gives you. Don't try to reinvent the wheel.

6: Go back to school. Take a class in tarot or any related subject, such as astrology, numerology, runes, I Ching, Kabbalah, dream interpretation, tea-leaf reading, meditation, palmistry, or chakra balancing. You might also want to take a class designed to help you express your creativity through drawing, painting, creative writing, or literature. Bring your new studies into your work with the cards, and document the results in your tarot journal.

7: Find a theme. Go back through your journal entries, and see what themes you can spot, as well as variations on those themes, just as you would during a tarot reading.

8: Be hateful. It's human nature to tend to be passionate in describing things that we hate. Find a card that makes you angry or fills you with disgust. Then get your creative juices flowing with a good old-fashioned rant. Vent, lash out, spout off, and rage on the page. What does the card—and your comments—tell you about yourself?

9: *Change your point of view*. Get a new perspective. Be like the Hanged Man: turn your journal over and write upside down, or rotate it ninety degrees and write sideways. Start in the middle of the page, and write in a circle or a spiral. If you are left-handed, write with your right hand.

10: *Switch voices*. If you normally write about yourself in the first person, with lots of "I's" and "me's," switch to third person— "he," "she," or "it."

11: *Tense up*. If you usually write in the past tense, try writing in the present or future tense, or the historical present, in which you would describe past events as though they were happening now: "The sun is shining brightly as I wait for the bus. It's my first day of school, and I'm excited—and scared, both."

12: *Switch styles*. If you normally write in longhand, try printing your entries. If you usually keep a handwritten journal, try typing instead.

13: *Switch hands*. Write with your non-dominant hand. If you are right-handed, use your left.

14: *Switch times*. Experiment with writing in the early morning, at lunch, after dinner, or just before bed.

15: *Switch formats*. Go from a bound book to a journaling program on your computer. Try dictating your journal into a tape recorder or videotaping yourself.

16: *Switch mediums*. Draw, paint, or collage your entry.

17: *Try a change of scene*. Try writing in a coffee shop, at the beach, in your car, or on the porch.

18: Go on a date. Julia Cameron, author of *The Artist's Way*, recommends a weekly "artist's date" in which you feed your creative spirit. Take a walk. Visit a museum. Treat yourself to a break that will refresh and recharge your artistic nature.

19: Go shopping. Buy new journaling supplies. Get new pens, markers, and colored pencils. Treat yourself to a scented candle or a new CD. Find a new deck of tarot cards to use with your journal.

20: Start over. Begin a new journal with a new theme and a renewed focus.

21: Journal with a friend. Arrange to meet in a restaurant, a coffee shop, a hotel lobby, or a park, and write side by side.

22: Retreat. Go on a journaling retreat, either alone or with others. Spend a full day or two journaling in the park, at a campground, at the library, or at a bed-and-breakfast. Who knows how far you could travel through the pages of your journal?

3
What Crowns You

Turn up the third card; place it above the Significator, and say: This crowns him. It represents (a) the Querent's aim or ideal in the matter; (b) the best that can be achieved under the circumstances, but that which has not yet been made actual.

—ARTHUR EDWARD WAITE,
The Pictorial Key to the Tarot (1910)

Personal Privacy and the Ethics of Keeping a Tarot Journal

In an ideal world, your tarot journal would always remain private. No one in your home would ever think of reading it without permission. Even if you accidentally left your journal wide open on the kitchen table, anyone who happened to pass by would just keep walking or close it gently and return it to you.

In the real world, however, tarot journals are a source of a wide range of ethical and privacy landmines. A tarot journal combines two intensely personal realms: the secret world of your inner thoughts and the private world of the tarot reading.

Writing About Readings

Tarot readings are intensely personal events. Even when tarot readings are conducted in the spirit of fun—at a party, for example, or after dinner with friends—surprisingly intimate issues are bound to come up. In fact, tarot readings can get so personal that many tarot readers refuse to allow onlookers—and they refuse to discuss individual tarot readings with anyone after the fact.

Does that mean you shouldn't write about a tarot reading? Will you violate anyone else's privacy if you keep a record of their readings?

There are a few simple steps you can take with your journal, both to protect other people's privacy and stay true to your own tarot-reading ethics.

Get permission. Ask permission before you write down any information about the tarot readings you conduct for other people. Tell them why you want to take notes in your journal and what you plan to do with those notes.

Write after the fact. Don't write in your journal while you're conducting a reading. You will inhibit the flow of information from the cards, and you will interrupt your conversation with your client. Make your journal entries at the conclusion of your readings; the cards on the table should be enough to refresh your memory about anything you discussed.

Keep open records. Offer to give other people a copy of your notes about their readings. You could even keep a few sheets of old-fashioned carbon paper handy, so you can give them instant copies of your journal entries.

Be obtuse. Use initials or pseudonyms, instead of real names, to identify the people you write about in your journal.

Be careful. If you include private information about other people in your tarot journal, be prepared to safeguard it with extraordinary care. Don't leave it where you might lose it, or where someone could pick it up and read it—like your desk at work or the coffee shop or the front seat of your car. When other people entrust you with their deeply held secrets, you have a moral and an ethical obligation to keep those secrets safe.

Reading About Others

What about using the cards to explore the role of other people in your own life? One of the most popular reasons for keeping a journal is to improve your relationships. You might be seeking insight into the motivations of people around you or examining their reactions to things you have said and done. Adding tarot cards to your journaling process will often help you recognize causes and connections that would otherwise go unnoticed by your conscious mind.

It can also be tempting to go to the cards for straight, immediate answers, without analysis.

You should know, however, that it can be hazardous to use tarot cards only to get information about other people—especially if you are seeking information that they wouldn't choose to share with you under normal circumstances. In fact, many experienced tarot readers think it's a serious violation of ethics to read tarot cards about anyone who hasn't given permission.

Likewise, it's a bad idea to use your journal to plumb the depths of what may be happening in other people's private lives, and you shouldn't use tarot cards to try to read someone else's thoughts or gauge their emotions. For one thing, the information you glean in a secret, unauthorized reading probably won't help you much. You won't get the full story—just as you wouldn't get the whole truth from rumors or gossip. What's more, in a measure of cosmic justice, you could soon find that other people in your life are going behind your back to get information about you.

There are times, of course, when you can ethically ask the cards about another person. The key is to make sure that your questions focus on your role in that person's life. It is perfectly okay, for example, to ask how someone perceives you, or feels about you, or will respond to something you say or do.

Ultimately, your goal should be to use tarot cards—and your tarot journal—to look for ways that you can help others and improve your relationships with them. Just make sure that you and your relationships with them are the real focus of the inquiry. Make sure that you are motivated by the right reasons, that you consider your questions carefully, and that you are willing to live with any repercussions.

In your tarot journal, as in any tarot practice, you will get the best results by examining your own role in your relationships. Limit your tarot readings to questions that directly pertain to your own life and your own thoughts. Focus your thoughts and energy on your own choices and your own past, present, and future. That way, the information you glean from a tarot reading will be properly focused on your own life.

Private Matters

If someone close to you might come across your tarot journal, you probably should take some steps to protect your privacy—as well as their feelings.

Post a "keep out" sign. If you think you can scare trespassers away, you might want to open your journal with a warning.

This is my private journal. Don't read it!

Open with a disclaimer. You want to put a disclaimer on the first page.

> *This journal is a private tool of introspection, reflection, and self-development. While the entries in this journal are based on the events and experiences of my everyday life, some of them are also imaginary. Some may be fantasy or fiction. Any similarities to actual events, places, and people may be entirely coincidental.*

Ultimately, you will probably have the most success if you take a few steps to ensure that your journal simply doesn't pose a temptation to passersby.

What's in a name? Call your tarot journal a notebook, and tell others you are using it in your study of the cards. Make it seem dry, scholarly, and of no more interest than a collection of chemistry notes.

Write in code. Use language that only you will understand, including initials, pseudonyms, abbreviations, and shorthand notes.

Plant a red herring. Keep two duplicate journals—a real one with your true thoughts and feelings, and a boring "bogus" journal to fake out any spies. You can fill it with grocery lists, weather reports, and reminders of things you need to do.

Keep your journal hidden. Don't leave your journal lying out in plain sight. Because you probably won't fool anyone by stashing your journal in your sock drawer, storing it in a desk drawer, or sliding it under your mattress, think of unusual hiding places. Wrap it in foil and keep it in your freezer. Lock it in the trunk of your car. Stash it in your toolbox. Just make sure you don't hide it so well that *you* can't find it.

Become a master of disguise. Cover your journal with a dust jacket from another book, and hide it in plain sight on your bookshelf.

Keep it locked. Desperate times may call for desperate measures. You can always drill a hole through your journal and padlock it. Or you can keep your journal in a fireproof home safe.

Go high-tech. Keep an electronic version of your journal on your computer. Use software that requires a password to open files. Encrypt your text or lock your documents so that no one can read them for a pre-set period of time.

Share the joy. Encourage others to start—and keep—their own journals right along with you.

Share with Care

Most people would agree that it is a violation of privacy and ethics to disclose other people's secrets. But what about sharing your own private thoughts or revealing your own secrets? Can you share your journal with other people? Should you?

It's a tricky question—and you might want to consider all of the ramifications before you make your life an open book.

Routine journal entries probably will never be an issue. If you simply want to share an account of your trip to Chicago, or a review of last night's movie, or your plans for an upcoming dinner party, you pose little risk of offending others or of opening yourself to criticism, judgment, or ridicule.

But you should be selective in what you choose to share, and any entry that reveals sensitive personal information should stay closely guarded.

Before you make any of your journal entries available to someone else, make sure that you trust them not to be hurt by what you have written—or to be overly critical of your views or hurtful in their response.

Also, know your own reasons for wanting to share. Are you looking for love? Understanding? A sympathetic ear? A shoulder to cry on? Whatever the reason, be clear about the reaction you want to solicit. You may or may not want feedback: say so up front. If you want comments, be specific about what kind of remarks you would like to hear.

Even if you keep an openly public journal, as many people do on the web, always remember that anyone with an Internet connection can access it. Don't post information that could damage your reputation, and be especially cautious about personal information you post about other people. A public journal is not the place to air your grievances with others or expose their failures and shortcomings.

A Legal Brief

If you are concerned about lawsuits or even just the possibility of finding yourself in court, you should know that journals and diaries can be subpoenaed. Your Fifth Amendment right not to incriminate yourself doesn't cover your journal entries, even if you believe them to be private. In fact, journals and diaries are routinely entered as evidence in court cases. If you are in a position in which you believe your words could be used against you in a court of law, consult an attorney.

Final Arrangements

What will you do with your journals when you finish working with them—or when you die? Should you burn them? Bury them? Throw them away? You might want to make arrangements for your ultimate parting of ways.

Many people plan for close friends, children, or grandchildren to inherit their journals—and, in fact, they write their journals with those audiences in mind.

You might also plan to donate your journals to a historical collection. Many colleges and universities maintain archives of historical documents, and personal journals and diaries are highly prized additions.

You may want to contribute journals to an archive in your home state. Materials there will be accessible to people who have an interest in the people, history, and culture of your area. If you are concerned about keeping secrets and maintaining confidentiality even after you are gone, you can ask that your journal be kept private for a period of years; viewing restrictions on personal documents are routine at most archival institutions.

4

What Grounds You

Turn up the fourth card; place it below the Significator, and say: This is beneath him. It shews the
foundation or basis of the matter, that which has
already passed into actuality and which the Significator has made his own.

—ARTHUR EDWARD WAITE,
The Pictorial Key to the Tarot (1910)

How to Use a Tarot Journal as a Foundation for Your Work with the Cards

Whether you use your tarot journal primarily to enhance your comprehension of the cards or to enhance your understanding of yourself, your success depends on your understanding of each individual card. One by one, as you work your way through all seventy-eight cards of the tarot deck, you will develop a deeper understanding of the cards—and of yourself.

This chapter will outline several ways you can use your journal as a foundation for your work with the cards—and it will describe quite a few journaling techniques, as well.

Card Interpretations

If you plan to use your tarot journal as a card interpretation hand-book, you can lay the groundwork with some simple journal entries.

Consult the user's guide. Some tarot readers start their journals by copying information about each card from the little white booklet that comes with most decks—known affectionately in tarot circles as the LWB. Such notes could serve as a spring-board for your own thoughts and interpretations of each card.

Make a list. If you are planning to keep detailed notes about each card, you might want to design a blank "template" page —a checklist of the items you want to include in your entries. That way, you can standardize your format, you can keep your notes consistent from card to card, and later you can find information more easily. You can find a sample template form in appendix V.

Consider the source. Remember to note the source of any new information you record in your tarot journal in case you need to refer to it later. Just jot down the source—whether you are including information from a book, a website, an article, or your own experiences with the cards. You might think you will remember where you learn things, but time has a way of erasing information that your journal can keep safe.

Leave room for dessert. Your interpretations and notes are bound to evolve and grow over time. Ultimately, your interpretations could evolve into freeform essays about the meanings of each card. As you become more familiar with each of the cards— through your reading, your writing, and your related experi-ences, such as guided meditations and visualizations—you may want to clarify or modify or expand your interpretations and definitions. You could plan to leave space to revisit each card later, or you could plan to add to later journals and entries.

Cluster

The clustering technique integrates the processes of both the creative right and the analytical left side of the brain. Clustering is fast. It's comprehensive. And in many respects, the clustering layout reflects the basic tarot spread, in which you can see connections and reflections and overlaps and permutations between cards.

To cluster, start by writing a single word or phrase in the center of a page. You can start with the name of a card, the name of a character in the card, or a word that describes an image, object, or symbol on the card.

Circle the central word or phrase, and then branch out by adding any related words, phrases, or terms that come to mind. Draw lines connecting your ideas. Free associate and head off on any tangents that interest you. Let your mind wander all over the page. You will probably find yourself making new and surprising connections, correlations, and associations—and connecting the dots in ways you never expected.

Later, you can use your clusters to develop keywords for individual cards. You can also use them as the basis of future journal entries.

Card Descriptions

When you study the tarot, much of your work will involve studying individual cards. By writing descriptions of each card in your tarot journal, you will see each card more clearly.

Diagram. Use words to diagram the elements of the card, starting with the central objects and working out toward the periphery. If you are working with the Ten of Wands, for example, you might try something like this: *man—ten wands—path—little house—rolling hills—blue sky.*

Describe the card. Describe the card with as much detail as you can muster. Write as if you were describing it to someone who can't see it. What images, symbols, or colors catch your eye? What is the significance of the suit, the element, the number, and the astrological correspondence? Are there any props in the picture? How are the figures standing, sitting, or gesturing?

> *The Queen of Cups is sitting on her throne, surrounded by calm, tranquil blue water. Her blonde hair seems to blow softly in a warm breeze. She gazes reflectively at the cup she holds in her hands . . .*

React to the card. Based on a first, casual impression, write down your reactions to a card. Then go a step further. What feelings or thoughts does the card evoke?

Familiar figures. Do you know anyone who reminds you of a particular card? Who? And why? How does that affect your interpretation of the card?

Same old, same old. How have you experienced the situations depicted in each card? Think of times in the past when you have felt like the character on the card, acted like the character on the card, or found yourself in a circumstance like the one pictured on the card.

Altered points of view. Change your vantage point. Describe the card from above, from the side, from below, or from behind. Describe the card from the point of view of someone inside the card. Describe the card as if you were the artist. Describe the card as if you were the omniscient god who created the world depicted in the card.

In the background. Write only about the landscape or the background of the card. Forget about the people who are pictured in the card, the props, or anything situated in the area. Focus on the setting.

Don't bother to knock. If your card pictures a building, even one far in the distance, imagine what it would be like to go inside. Wander through the hallways, walk through the rooms, look in closets and cubbyholes. Look out of the windows. What will you see? What will you discover?

Hike the back country. Picture yourself wandering through the landscape of the tarot cards. Wade into the streams. Swim in the lakes. Climb the trees. Discover where the road leads. Where does the river flow? What is just over the horizon? Who else will you meet inside the card? Record your amblings and adventures.

Dip into a stream of consciousness. Many tarot cards depict bodies of water. Examine your card. Do you see a pond, a lake, or a sea? A stream or a river? What color is the water? Is it moving or still? What is going on beneath the surface? Step into the water. How do you move? Do you wade or swim? How do your feelings change as a result of your dip? Write it all down.

Location, location, location. Have you ever been to a place like the location pictured on the card? How did you get there? What did you do there? Who else was there? Who did you meet? What kind of person were you then? How did that place change you? How has time changed you? What would you expect if you went back?

A change of seasons. Change the seasons in a card. If flowers are blooming and trees are budding, imagine the same environment in autumn or winter. How does the change of seasons affect the characters in the card?

Natural development. Imagine that you will develop the natural setting of a card. Who will move in, and why? What will they build? How will they use the land?

One Card a Day

Many tarot readers draw one card a day, both for study and for reflection. One-card readings focus on a single moment in time and force you to recognize critical, immediate information. One-card readings can be routine or reflective, as quick or intense as you like, but they do tend to force you to go deep into yourself for insight and answers.

Card-a-day readings, like the phases of the moon, are fluid and constantly evolving. They can reveal slivers of insight or illuminate a full circle of information. A card-a-day reading can be a learning aid, as you work your way progressively through all seventy-eight cards. A card-a-day reading can be a predictive tool, as you seek omens and augurs, predictions and forecasts for the day that is about to unfold. A card-a-day reading can help you measure and hone your intuition. A card-a-day reading can also be a meditative device or a jumping-off point for creative inspiration and journal entries.

Keeping a card-a-day journal is simple.

Pick a card. When you first wake up, shuffle and draw a card at random. Keep the card in mind—or keep it with you—as you go through the day. If you normally carry your journal with you, you could tuck the card into its pages. You could glue an envelope to the inside cover, just to hold your card of the day. You could even paperclip your card to one of the pages. At the end of the day, make notes about your observations.

First thing in the morning, draw a single card at random and see how many of the symbols in the card pop up during the course of your day. Watch for parallels between the cards you draw, the people you meet, and the events of the day. Your sharp-tongued coworker, for example, might be the Queen of Swords; an unexpected job assignment could be the Ten of Wands.

Before you go to bed, note your card—and the events of the day—in your journal. As you write, ask yourself how you feel about each card. Can you change your attitude and make a Ten of Wands seem like an Ace of Wands?

Enter it in the log. Additionally, you might want to use your card-a-day journal to maintain a checklist-style log of the cards you have drawn. At a glance, you can see which cards you have drawn repeatedly, which cards are most prominent during different phases of your life, and which cards are notable by their absence. Cards that either show up repeatedly or fail to make an appearance are equally telling. List all of the cards in the deck, from the Fool to the King of Pentacles. Draw lines to create a grid or leave space to record the date each card is drawn. Leave a page to keep a daily reading chart. List cards with check boxes and date boxes. (You can find a sample checklist in appendix V.)

The end of the day. You don't have to choose your card of the day in the morning, at random. You can also select your card consciously and face up at the end of the day. Just look through the cards and find one that seems to summarize or capture the spirit and events of the day that is now drawing to a close.

Today was an Eight of Wands day for me. The phone didn't stop ringing once. Every time I'd hang up, someone else would call. You'd think I was the only person in the office who could handle

the customers. A lot of it was coworkers transferring calls to me.
The fax kept ringing, too, and my e-mail was out of control. I
know the Eight of Wands is supposed to represent long-distance
and electronic communication, but this was ridiculous. I missed
lunch, and I couldn't even get to the bathroom.

Correspondences

Any serious study of the tarot would be incomplete without noting
the myriad correspondences and cross-references that tarot scholars
have developed over the centuries. For example, the four suits of
the Minor Arcana—wands, cups, swords, and pentacles—correspond
to the four suits of an ordinary playing card deck (clubs, hearts,
spades, and diamonds), the four ancient elements (fire, water, air, and
earth), and the four realms of human existence (spiritual, emotional,
intellectual, and physical).

Correspondences give us a sense of structure, of design, of deep-
rooted foundation in our work with the cards. Correspondences
help us recognize that the structure of the tarot deck is not arbitrary. The framework is not haphazard. Tarot is not coincidence.
There is a sensibility and symmetry to the structure of the deck.
Correspondences help us make sense not only of the cards but also
of our lives.

You can enter correspondences as you discover them. You may
want to reserve several pages strictly to record your correspondence
guide in list or table form. See appendix II for an example.

Symbolic Touches

The tarot, which was born in Renaissance Italy and spread through
France, is inextricably linked to the culture and tradition of Western
Europe. The cards are steeped in the myths of Greece and Rome,
the Bible, and the history of Europe and the Americas. As a result,

many of the tarot's images and symbols hold standard meanings that are readily understood by anyone familiar with Western culture. Most, for example, could immediately relate to the idea that an apple symbolizes "forbidden fruit," and they could extrapolate a wide range of related implications from the image.

You can find standard symbols and their interpretations listed in symbol dictionaries. Occasionally, however, tarot artists and designers add new layers of interpretation to their cards, so symbolism sometimes varies from artist to artist, deck to deck.

More importantly, your own interpretations may vary from anything an artist intended. Sometimes, an image or detail may not be universally regarded as a symbol—but it may hold symbolic significance for you.

You might want to use your tarot journal to help you develop a personalized symbol dictionary, both to note symbols that may be unique to your deck and to note symbols that hold special significance for you. Pay special attention to symbols and imagery that crop up in the cards and in your everyday life. When you see a black cat skulking across your yard, for example, then that cat reappears in your dreams, and then you notice a black cat on the Queen of Wands, your own observations and interpretations of the symbol will be more relevant than anything you could find in a published symbol dictionary.

Keep a list of symbols you see in the cards, along with related symbols you notice during the course of your everyday life. You can look up their meanings in symbol dictionaries, along with whatever individual or personal meaning they hold for you.

Spreads and Layouts

As you work with tarot cards, you will naturally move between one-card spreads and larger spreads like the Celtic Cross. You might learn spreads from other readers, and you will probably even develop spreads of your own, in response to specific questions and follow-up inquiries.

You can use your journal to keep a record of spreads you have learned and spreads you invent. Just draw a quick sketch or diagram of each position in the spread and its significance.

Character Sketches

The characters in the tarot are much more than paper dolls or cardboard cutouts. Because each one is based on powerful archetypes and symbols, they seem to come to life with very little effort. As you meet and work with each one through the pages of your tarot journal, you will find that they all have stories to tell, adventures to share, and lessons to teach.

Life stories. Pick a character in any card, at random, or choose one that you would like to know better. Take the ferryman in the Six of Swords, for example. Name him, give him a life history, and describe what is happening to him in the card. Explore his past, present, and future, at length. Ultimately, you may discover that what you think about a character can tell you a lot about yourself.

Fiction writers often create elaborate histories and profiles of the characters in their stories. Here are some factors you might like to consider in order to transform your tarot characters from two-dimensional figures into full-figured, well-rounded personalities.

- Name
- Age
- Address
- Physical description: eye color, weight, height, predominant feature, scars, tattoos, or distinguishing marks

- Strengths, weaknesses, and vulnerabilities
- Habits, good and bad
- Pet peeves
- Talents and hobbies
- Life history: birth date, astrological sign, hometown, earliest memory, education, adolescence
- Family: parents, brothers and sisters, uncles, aunts, and grandparents
- Home life: spouse, children, pets
- Close contacts: best friends, advisors, enemies, employers, supervisors, coworkers
- Employment: current job, work history, responsibilities, salary
- Daily routine
- Favorite things: vacation spot, color, music, food, restaurant, shops and stores, book, magazine, movie, television show, sayings and expressions

A day in the life. Describe a day in the life of a figure in a card. What do they do when they wake up? How do they prepare for the day? What takes up most of their time? With whom do they eat, work, play, and spend the night?

Age progression. Try your hand at age progression and regression. Describe what a character will be like when they are twenty years older or, alternately, what they were like twenty years ago.

Job search. Write a résumé for a character in the cards. Invent and include their full name, address, objective, education, experience, expertise, and references.

Pen pals. Write a letter to a figure in a card or from a figure in the card. It can be any type of letter: a job application, news to an old friend, e-mail. Imagine that you are the character in the card and write a letter to yourself. Write a letter to a character in a card that you don't understand, don't like, do like, or want to know more about. Say anything and everything you want; ask questions. Then answer the letter you wrote as if you were the character. You can also compose entries in the form of telegrams and e-mail.

Play matchmaker. Find characters from different cards. Look for characters that seem compatible, as well as pairs that would be completely at odds. Set them up on a date, arrange for them to be invited to the same party, or make them coworkers. Put them on the bus or the subway together, or trap them in an elevator for an hour. Observe how they get along, and record your observations.

Change of scene. Remove a figure from one card and insert them into another. Put the Hanged Man on the Hermit's mountain. Have Temperance take a test drive in the Chariot.

How do the characters' perspectives change? What advice do they have to offer from their new location?

Prop master. Find an image in a card. Now find one in real life. Hold it. Write about it. Make it a real, tangible experience.

Borrowed clothing. Borrow a set of clothing from one of the characters in the card. Write about how it makes you feel.

Someone else's shoes. Choose any figure from any card—man, woman, child, or animal. Slip into her body. Slip into his skin. Look out at the world through her eyes. Feel his body—bone, muscle, and skin. Feel her clothing. Move around. Stand, sit, walk, run, and stretch. Look at his reflection in a mirror. Imagine that you are the main character in the card.

How are you standing or sitting? How does that feel, spiritually, emotionally, intellectually, and physically? Are you holding anything? What? What does it feel like? What does it symbolize? Write down all of your impressions in your journal.

Trading places. Imagine that you can trade places with any figure in any card. Who would you switch places with—and why? What will you do first? What do you do? How do you do it? And what advice would you have for the character who will fill your shoes for the day?

Be the ball. See yourself as the figure on the card—not an idealized version of yourself and not someone in a costume. Picture yourself in the card, exactly as you are, right now, and write a description of how you look and feel.

Go Inside the Cards

Sometimes, people who study tarot cards imagine themselves inside the cards, exploring the landscape and meeting personally with the characters inside each card. Typically, they enter each card through meditations and visualizations—two simple, remarkably effective ways to connect personally with each card.

The two techniques work seamlessly to bridge the communication gap between your conscious and subconscious minds. Because the information you glean during a meditation comes directly from your subconscious mind, it is imminently relevant and pertinent to your life. And because your journeys occur when you are fully conscious, meditations are easy to remember when you're through. Simply allow your mind to wander, and watch as events unfold on the page.

A Guide to Guided Meditation

You may want to try guided meditation before you work in your tarot journal. Guided meditation will calm you and make it possible to explore the cards in depth.

Once you start using guided meditation regularly, you might be surprised at how quickly you can attain a state of altered consciousness. Many people, relaxed by deep breathing and stillness, find that they can slip into a meditative state simply by allowing their bodies to rest and their minds to wander.

You might also be surprised by how "real" guided meditation feels. With your eyes closed, you might see vivid images in your mind. You might hear sounds, either subtle or dramatic. You might even notice odors, tastes, and the sensation of different textures against your skin. Some of it may seem literal. Other aspects of your experience might register more as impressions, feelings, or intuitive flashes.

If guided meditation doesn't work for you right away, don't panic. It might take practice. At first, you might not see any images. You might not hear, smell, or taste anything. In fact, you will probably notice your impressions come most clearly in one format: usually sight, sound, or smell.

Enjoy whatever you do experience. Each time you practice, you will get better.

The following all-purpose meditation will work with any tarot card. You can use it with a card you pick at random. You can also choose to use it with a card you especially like or one you dislike intensely.

For best results, have someone read this aloud to you, or tape-record it for yourself.

The Meditation

Choose your card, and examine it carefully for sixty seconds. Start with the name and number of the card. Then look at the sky pictured in the card, and let your gaze move down the card, across the landscape. Notice the background of the card, and then shift your attention to the foreground. Pay attention to every detail. What colors are most prominent? Are there people in the card? How are they standing or sitting? How are they dressed? What are they holding? What are the expressions on their faces? Are there animals in the card? What are they doing? In short, try to memorize the full scope of the card.

Now close your eyes, but keep the card in mind.

Sit comfortably, with both feet solidly grounded on the floor. Make sure there is nothing in your lap and nothing in your hands. Breathe deeply, three times. Breathe in through your nose, and breathe out through your mouth. Remember to keep breathing deeply throughout this meditation.

[Pause.]

Relax completely, starting with your feet. Wiggle your toes and then relax them. Flex your ankles and relax your feet. Relax your calves, relax your knees, and relax your thighs. Relax your hips and settle comfortably in your chair. Take a deep breath and relax your stomach. Wiggle your fingers and then relax them. Relax your hands, your wrists, and your arms. Shrug your shoulders and then relax them. Move your head in a gentle circle and relax your neck. Unclench your teeth, relax your jaw, and take another deep breath. Notice how the deep breathing helps you sharpen your concentration and focus your attention.

[Pause.]

Keep your eyes closed. Continue to breathe deeply, and see the card again in your mind's eye. Reconstruct it completely, from top to bottom. As you envision the card, see it as large as life, filling the landscape in front of you. The borders of the card will become a doorway, and a shining path will lead from your feet through that doorway, into the card.

Follow that path, and walk slowly and comfortably into the card.

[Pause.]

Look around. Notice the view in front of you, as well as to your right and to your left.

Keep breathing deeply, and become increasingly aware of your surroundings.

What do you see?

What do you hear?

What is the weather like?

How does it feel to be inside the card?

[Pause.]

Now look around until you find a character from the card. Approach that figure. He or she has been expecting you, and he or she has something to say to you.

Take a moment, and listen carefully.

[Pause.]

If you have any questions, feel free to ask them. You may or may not get a response. You may spend a few moments in quiet conversation, or you may get an unspoken, symbolic message. Take a few moments to communicate.

[Pause.]

It is almost time to say goodbye and come back to this room. Offer your thanks, and then start moving away. As you leave, remember that you can return to the card at any time by relaxing and remembering the route you took into the card.

[Pause.]

Take a long, final look around the card. Then see the doorway that you used to enter the card, the doorway back to this room.

Walk back through the doorway to this room. Step through the doorway, and get ready to come back to your life in the real world. With your eyes still closed, take three deep breaths to catch up to the here and now. With each breath, you will feel more awake and reinvigorated. Take two more deep breaths, and when you are ready, open your eyes.

Journaling Prompts

- What did you first notice about your surroundings?
- What did you see when you looked down at the ground?
- What caught your eye when you looked out at the landscape?
- What did you hear?
- What time of day was it?
- What was the temperature like, and how did the air feel against your skin?
- Of all sensations you experienced, which was the strongest?
- What were you wearing?
- Who did you encounter in the card?
- Can you describe that figure? Describe their dress, posture, expression, and mannerisms.
- What message did that figure have for you?
- How does this message relate to your life at this moment?
- Did this meditation hold any surprises for you?
- What did you like or dislike the most about your experience?
- Would you like to return to this meditation on your own? Why or why not?

Focused Meditation

Once you become proficient at guided meditation, you can also enter a card simply by looking at it.

Preparation. Choose one card from the deck. Sit comfortably in a chair, with your feet firmly on the floor, and breathe deeply. As you breathe, relax and study the card in front of you. Examine every detail. As you look at the card, imagine it growing larger and larger, until it stands in front of you, like a doorway into another world. Picture yourself walking through that doorway and into the card.

Survey the grounds. Look around, and describe what you see. What do you notice that you couldn't see from outside the card? What do you hear? What do you smell? What is the weather like? How does it feel to be inside the card?

You will probably be surprised by what you can sense. Many people who try this meditate with the cards or visualize themselves entering a card and report hearing background noise like wind, birds, and waves. They can feel the heat of the sun or a cool breeze or the grass underneath their feet. They can even smell flowers, grass, and salty sea air.

You're not alone. You find yourself face to face with a character from the card. Write about the experience. Where do you meet her? What is he wearing? What is the expression on her face? What is his mood? How does she react to your presence? Does he greet you, or must you initiate a conversation? What does she say to you? How do you respond? Does he have a message for you? Does she have a gift for you? What is it? How do you feel about it? What do you say to him? What will you remember most about your encounter?

The safe haven. Imagine that you are on the run from an unseen attacker. Suddenly you find yourself in the scene shown in your card, where you can hide safely. What makes this card a refuge for you? What help can you find here? Put it down on paper.

Unexpected visitors. You may have gone into the cards during meditation or visualization in order to explore the world of the tarot from the perspective of the cards. Now, try the process in reverse. Imagine that one of the characters has come out of a card to meet you in your surroundings. Imagine finding the Magician in your kitchen, or the boys from the Five of Wands roughhousing in your living room, or the Hanged Man at your computer.

Visualize yourself walking through your front door and going through your house until you find your visitor. How do you feel? Angry? Alarmed? Amused? What will you say? What will the two of you talk about? Record your interaction in your journal.

Tour guide. Imagine that one of the figures from a tarot card is staying with you as a houseguest. What will you do to entertain your guest? Where will you take him? What will you share with her? How will he react?

Dialogues

Dialogues are imaginary conversations that take place only in your mind or in the pages of your journal. All you need to do is start the conversational ball rolling—metaphorically speaking—and write down the exchange exactly as you imagine it.

You can create a dialogue with any person, place, or thing. You can imagine a dialogue with any creature or image in any tarot card: the apprentice in the Eight of Pentacles, the dog that nips at the heels of the Fool, the snake in the tree behind the Lovers, or the four sunflowers in the Sun card. You can even imagine a dialogue between two characters, two cards, or two versions of the same card.

The process is as unlimited as your imagination. If you are willing to recognize that the tarot allows the flow of symbolic information from your subconscious mind—and roll with that flow—you can get results.

Here are some starting ideas.

Ask questions. Don't start with any suppositions or expectations. Just pose a question to any card you choose, and wait for the answer. Even if the response doesn't make sense, ask for clarification and write it all down. The process is kind of like channeling, in which cosmic wisdom and information is said to come from otherworldly entities.

Ask for information. Ask the figures in the cards for background information, names, dates, places, and details. You can even use your best investigator's impersonation: "Just the facts, ma'am."

Ask for advice. Seek guidance, counsel, and advice from a trusted ally in the cards, either one that you choose deliberately or one who seems to show up repeatedly in your readings and journaling sessions.

Eavesdrop. Observe and record as characters from two different cards talk to each other.

Interview. There may be times during your pursuit of information and knowledge, both of yourself and of the cards, when you will feel like a journalist who is on the trail of a big story. Tarot cards can lend you an inside scoop on practically any subject.

It is easy to follow a reporter's format as you investigate. Just refer to the "Five W's"—who, what, when, where, and why—and how. Keep asking those questions. The first answer you receive might not always be self-explanatory. Dig deep. You might find yourself uncovering breaking news or the story of a lifetime.

Lists

Writer Anthony Burgess once said that given a choice between a new play by Shakespeare and a grocery list from the famous playwrite, he'd want the grocery list, for its ability to illuminate the man a little more.

Lists are telling, descriptive, and quick. They lend insight into your daily life, as well as your motivations, drives, and desires.

Make a list of all the symbols on every card. You do not need to define or interpret them right away. Simply note their presence on each card.

Lists you can create include:

Keywords of words and phrases, definitions, and information about each card in the tarot deck.

Top tens. List ten things about a card. You can take them directly from the card or they may simply be inspired by the card. You could list quotes, song titles, symbols, colors, impressions, or anything you like.

Colorful language. Write a list of adjectives that describe each card: big, small, bright, hot, dim, or scintillating.

To be, or not to be. Write a list of "is" and "is not" qualities for each card.

Question authority. Make a list of questions you hear frequently about the tarot.

Routine inquiries. Make a list of questions people commonly ask during their readings, along with your answers.

Pros and cons. List the positives and negatives, the pros and cons, of each card.

Likes and dislikes. List the things you like and dislike about each card.

Quotations. Keep a list of quotes that remind you of the cards.

Songs. Keep a list of songs that remind you of the cards.

Gratitudes. Use the cards to remind you of your blessings and things for which you are grateful.

Timed Writing

Timed writing is a staple of many journaling programs. When you try timed writing, it doesn't matter what you write; your only goal is to start writing, and keep writing, until your time is up.

Timed writing sessions force you to write without overanalyzing your efforts or doubting your talents. Timed writing helps unblock your communication skills and primes the pump for further work.

There are several types of timed writing.

Less is more. Limited timed writing means you must stop when the timer goes off.

Icebreaker. If you are using timed writing as a prompt, you can keep going for as long as you like.

Focused free writing. Select a card you wish to explore. Set a timer for five, ten, or fifteen minutes. Look at the card and start writing whatever comes to mind. At first, your entries may seem like complete nonsense—but don't pause or stop, and don't edit or rewrite your entries. Don't cross out words, second-guess your spelling, or feel self-conscious about your storytelling ability. If you need to, think of your journal as a rough draft. Just keep your pen moving.

If you can't think of anything new to say, repeat something you just wrote, or write, "I can't think of anything to write." If you find yourself going off on tangents, that's okay, too. Just keep writing, no matter what comes to mind.

An hour of your time. Set aside an hour, and write about one single card for at least sixty minutes. When you think you have run out of things to write, keep going. You might say, "That's all I see. A tree, a rock." Keep writing until you have thoroughly described and examined a single card.

When your time has elapsed, go back over your work and underline the words, phrases, and sentences you find most meaningful.

Creative Writing

The tarot can be a useful tool for amateur and professional writers alike. Sometimes, when you lay out the cards, stories practically write themselves. Rachel Pollack and Caitlin Matthews used tarot cards to inspire a wide range of authors to contribute to their anthology, *Tarot Tales*. Martin H. Greenberg and Lawrence Schimel also compiled an innovative collection of short stories entitled *Tarot Fantastic*.

You can use tarot cards to create any style of fiction, poetry, or drama, or to enhance your understanding of literature by others.

Casting couch. Use the characters from your favorite book to stand in as the lead players of your own tarot deck, much like the creators of *The Wonderland Tarot Deck* or *The Tarot of Oz*. You can also cast tarot figures in your favorite television show or movie.

Myths and fairy tales. Select cards that reflect the characters and the story lines of classic myths and fairy tales, like Liz Greene and Juliet Sharman-Burke did with *The Mythic Tarot*, and Anna-Marie Ferguson did with *Legend: The Arthurian Tarot*.

At the movies. Think about a story or movie you know well, and connect various characters and events with an appropriate card. Pick additional cards to serve as storyboards depicting locations, plot twists, climax, and resolution.

The power of three. Choose three images, symbols, or impressions—at random—from one card. Use them in a sentence, and use that sentence to begin a story.

A work of fiction. Tarot cards can be a secret weapon in the creative writer's arsenal. The cards can suggest characters, conflict, crisis, and resolution. Start simply, by writing a single sentence based on the tarot. Choose three highlights from any card: a color, an object, or an expression, for example. Then use two of those highlights in a sentence. Then use that sentence as the first sentence of a short story.

You can create characters based on the cards, derive plot twists from random tarot readings, and find conclusions in the outcome card of any spread. You can even generate dialogue by using the same dialogue techniques you use in your journal.

Poetry in motion. Write a poem about a card. Initial poems are fairly easy: just use the letters of any tarot-related word—like "moon," for example—as the first letter in each line of your poem. You might like to try your hand at haiku, a Japanese style of poetry, traditionally written in three lines of five, seven, and five syllables each. You could even write a tarot limerick or a tarot nursery rhyme.

Artistic Pursuits

Illuminate your journal. You can create an illuminated journal, like the monks during medieval times who embellished the large initials at the beginning of a page and illustrated the margins with intricate designs and miniature images. Start by painting colorful borders on some—or all—of the pages of your journal, even before you begin to write. Stock up on scrapbooking supplies at your local arts and crafts shop. As you compose your journal entries, try sketching or drawing a few illustrations to accompany your writing. Color your artwork with markers or colored pencils.

A picture is worth a thousand words. You can even forget writing completely and create a visual journal. You can express yourself through watercolor paintings, pen-and-ink sketches, pencil drawings, or any artistic medium you like.

Piece it together. Even if you don't feel like much of an artist, you can collage. Use an inexpensive foam paintbrush to coat a few pages with gesso (available from art supply shops). Tear colored tissue paper and glue it onto the pages with adhesive or gel. Cut images and illustrations from magazines, along with words and letters that seem to reflect your thoughts and feelings. Sprinkle your creations with glitter, and embellish your work with bits of fabric, feathers, glitter, and rubber stamps. You can even add copper, gold, or metallic leafing.

Design your own deck. Most people who work with tarot cards can usually find a tarot deck they like—one that resonates with their worldview, speaks their language, sings to their soul. After a while, however, one or two cards might start to feel a little off. You might think the miser in the Four of Pentacles looks a little too stingy, or wish you could trim that scruffy beard on the King of Wands. In fact, almost everyone who works with tarot cards eventually starts to think about the deck they would create for themselves—if only they had the time and the talent.

Your tarot journal is the place to start sketching and listing ideas for your own perfect deck. In fact, Arnell Ando's work in her journal led to the creation of her deck, *The Transformational Tarot*.

First, gather your journaling art supplies, such as markers, glitter pens, scissors, and glue. Find a healthy supply of old magazines, preferably ones printed on heavy coated stock. (Fashion magazines and catalogs have the best pictures of people, and travel magazines have the best scenery. *National Geographic* magazines have both, and most used bookstores sell them for just pennies.) If you would like to include pictures of family, friends, and pets, find snapshots that you don't mind cutting apart.

Then go through your magazines, looking for images that appeal to you and reflect your understanding of the tarot. As you create your deck, focus on one card at a time. Concentrate on its meaning as you rifle through your images. You will probably be surprised at how quickly you will find the appropriate elements for your collage.

As you cut and paste each card, keep your favorite deck handy for inspiration or refer to a book like Anthony Louis's *Tarot Plain and Simple*. You might want to refer to your tarot deck to develop a list of images and symbols to use as a starting point for your search.

Sketching. Copy a card into your tarot journal. Don't trace: draw it freehand. You can use stick figures, if you like. Include important symbols, props, and details. You can even add talk balloons and thought bubbles, like a cartoon.

Etch a sketch. Copy a card without lifting your pen from the paper. The constant movement of your pen simulates the act of writing, lets your subconscious and conscious minds connect, and allows ideas and inspirations to flow.

Sweet Dreams

When you read tarot cards, you will be more open to messages and suggestions from your subconscious mind. Not only will you find yourself slipping into a dreamlike state when you read cards or write in your tarot journal, but you might also find that your dreams are set in the landscape of the tarot. You might even expect nighttime visits from the figures in the cards, as Major and Minor Arcana characters make guest appearances in your dreams. You might find yourself drinking with the innkeeper from the Nine of Cups or kneeling at the feet of the Hierophant.

A tarot journal is a good place to record your dreams, because many of the same symbols and archetypes that make up the images of each card also appear to us when we sleep.

Get ready for bed. You can even go so far as to plant the seeds of tarot dreams and visions. Make sure you have your journal and a good pen on your nightstand. Choose a single card at night, just before you go to sleep. Study it carefully. Tell yourself that you will receive insight and a message in a dream. When you wake up the next morning, write down the messages you receive. Cluster images and words to get them on paper fast. It might help to set your alarm to a quiet station or musical selection, so you won't be jolted into full consciousness. Also, write in semi-darkness or low light, so you can linger halfway in the world of your dreams.

5
What Lies Behind You

Turn up the fifth card; place it on the side of the
Significator from which he is looking, and say:
This is behind him. It gives the influence that is
just passed, or is now passing away.

—ARTHUR EDWARD WAITE,
The Pictorial Key to the Tarot (1910)

How to Rewrite History in the Pages of Your Journal

"Sometimes," said author Josephine Hart, "we need a map of the past. It helps us to understand the present and to plan the future."

Many people think of tarot cards as a tool for telling the future. In practice, however, tarot readers spend as much time looking backward as they do looking forward.

The future, after all, is vague, shapeless, and unformed. For most of us, it's too huge and too far away to picture clearly. At the same time, the present is fleeting. But the past is a place we recognize, and it's a place we're comfortable in—if only because it's familiar. We've been in the past. We lived through it. We know what happened . . . even if we don't always know why events unfolded as they did or how things came to pass.

That's where a tarot journal can help.

With your tarot cards on the table and your journal in hand, you can relive, reconsider, and re-create an entire lifetime—or maybe just an evening or two.

History in the Making

No one is able to move fully into the future until he or she is comfortable with what happened in the past.

When you can see the patterns and images of your past literally laid out in front of you, you can identify pivotal moments. By studying and re-examining your past, you can see the turning points in your life. You can spot cause and effect; you can see how a thought, a word, a look, or a gesture changed the course of events and set a new future into motion.

You can also use the experiences of the past to judge the present and make decisions for the future.

You can use your tarot journal to relive happy times and celebrate your past success. "We write to taste life twice," Anaïs Nin said, "in the moment and in retrospection."

You can even take ownership of all that has made you the person you are today.

A tarot journal can help you understand and heal old wounds. You can gain understanding, closure, and resolution. You can learn to let go of hurt and angry feelings.

Reviewing your past also demonstrates that you are not always a hapless victim of circumstance. You are the master of your own fate, the captain of your own ship, and, ultimately, the only one in complete control of your destiny.

In a tarot reading, the cards that fall in the past position serve as a measure of reliability. You can recognize events and experiences, and verify the cards' accuracy. By studying the cards' version of the past, you can also learn to decipher the symbolism of the tarot.

A tarot journal can also serve as a record of the person you are today, to serve as a reference for your future self—the person you will be tomorrow. "History will be kind to me," Winston Churchill once said, "for I intend to write it."

Here are some suggestions for dealing with your past in a tarot journal.

Study the Fool's Journey

The twenty-two cards of the Major Arcana combine to form an allegorical description of our journey through life. That adventure is frequently called the Fool's journey, in honor of the Fool card that leads the pack, representing each and every one of us.

In theory, the Fool moves step-by-step through each stage of human development, in order. In real life, however, most of us don't proceed sequentially. As you will see in your tarot readings, we move up and down, as well as back and forth. Sometimes we learn the lessons life tries to teach us. Sometimes we ignore them. Sometimes we forget—or fail—and we need to repeat a class.

Pull the Fool card from the deck, and lay the remaining Major Arcana cards, one through twenty-one, in three rows. Each row will have seven cards.

Then look at them from two perspectives—both as a series of consecutive lessons, and also as a cosmic game of "Chutes and Ladders."

Here are some suggestions for a very basic interpretation of each step of the journey. Feel free to change them, expand them, or adapt them to your own experience.

The Fool's Journey

ROW ONE

ROW TWO

ROW THREE

THE TWENTY-TWO CARDS OF THE MAJOR ARCANA, THE FOOL'S JOURNEY, LAID OUT
IN GROUPS OF SEVEN (USING THE UNIVERSAL TAROT BY ROBERTO DE ANGELIS).

Row One

*The Magician • The High Priestess • The Empress • The
Emperor • The Hierophant • The Lovers • The Chariot*

The first seven cards in the tarot often depict a fundamental level of development. They portray the earliest stages of self-awareness, our first relationships with others, and our initial attempts at self-mastery.

- With the Magician card, we discover our power to control the forces of nature and the world around us.
- The High Priestess may describe our early emotional life.
- The Empress may represent our mother.
- The Emperor might represent our father.
- The Hierophant might represent the beginning of our formal education and a growing awareness of societal expectations.
- The Lovers card depicts our first fumbling forays into romance.
- And the Chariot card describes our first independent travels out into the world. It's the "driver's permit" card.

Row Two

*Strength • The Hermit • The Wheel of Fortune • Justice •
The Hanged Man • Death • Temperance*

Refining our sense of self becomes more of an issue in the next seven cards of the tarot. They depict the challenges we face as we try to bend the world to our will.

- With the Strength card, we become heartened; our courage takes shape, and we become a force to be reckoned with.
- With the Hermit, we become more introspective.

- With the Wheel of Fortune, we begin to experience the seemingly random twists of fate. We discover that life often seems unfair.
- With Justice, we become more socially aware. We try to combat the unfairness of the Wheel of Fortune experience.
- With the Hanged Man, we learn the value of self-sacrifice for causes larger than ourselves.
- With Death, we learn how to make graceful transitions.
- And with Temperance, we learn how to mix and balance seemingly apparent forces.

Row Three

The Devil • The Tower • The Star • The Moon • The Sun • Judgement • The World

The universe has its own agenda, and once we let go of our attempt to control the whole world we truly realize our full potential.

- With the Devil, we learn of temptation, materialism, and the thrill of danger.
- With the Tower, we learn the consequences of poor choices—and we get the chance to rebuild.
- With the Star, we find new hope and set new goals for our lives.
- With the Moon, we learn how to best tame our primal urges.
- With the Sun, we rediscover our optimism and sense of self.
- With Judgement, we accept all of our mistakes and successes.
- With the World, we celebrate the full scope of our lives and prepare to begin a new cycle of learning and discovery.

Your Own Fool's Journey

Retrace your steps. Lay out the Major Arcana cards, and think back to a time in your life when you experienced each one of the archetypes firsthand. Keep the cards in order, but know that you don't have to list your own experiences in chronological order. It is perfectly okay to list an incident from your childhood right next to an event that took place during your first year of college. For example:

0. The Fool—I backpacked across Europe during the summer of my senior year.

1. The Magician—I learned to write.

2. The High Priestess—In tenth-grade English, Sister Mary Margaret taught me to love great books.

3. The Empress—I became a mother when Lizzie was born.

4. The Emperor—After just six months on the job, I was promoted to supervisor.

5. The Hierophant—I had a disagreement with our minister and I stopped going to church.

6. The Lovers—I fell in love for the first time when I met Steve.

7. The Chariot—I drove across the country for my first job.

8. Strength—I moved into my own apartment and got a pet cat.

9. The Hermit—I felt isolated and alone when I first moved to Colorado.

10. The Wheel of Fortune—I won a new TV in a department store raffle.

11. Justice—I got into a fender bender and the insurance company took me to court.

12. The Hanged Man—I felt like I was in suspended animation while I waited for the birth of my daughter.

13. Death—My grandfather died a month after Lizzie was born.

14. Temperance—I learned to balance my own needs with the needs of my family.

15. The Devil—I watched my brother become an alcoholic, and I watched him fight to recover.

16. The Tower—My house burned down.

17. The Star—I tried out for the school play when I was in tenth grade.

18. The Moon—As a teenager, I used to write poems in my room at night.

19. The Sun—I think my truest joy is watching my daughter as she plays outside.

20. Judgement—I willingly allowed my master's thesis to be judged by committee.

21. The World—I graduated with honors.

Tarot timelines. Alternately, you can create a timeline of your life and assign a tarot card to each significant milestone. You can also construct timelines for individual, more focused periods of time, such as your childhood, your adolescence, your college years, your career, or your marriage. You can chronicle your emotional development, your spiritual growth, your education and intellectual development, your physical growth, your health, or your aging process. You can even try variations on a theme by creating tarot timelines of your emotional, spiritual, intellectual, and physical development. Focus on your childhood, adolescence, high school and college years. Depict the life story of your marriage, your life as a parent, or your career.

Dateline. Make lists of important days, events, and milestones in your life—such as births, deaths, miscarriages, illnesses, injuries, moves, important meetings, interviews, and graduations. Do your best to develop a comprehensive record of your life and times. Because it could take some time to remember all of your milestones, leave space so that you can add dates as you remember them.

Remembrance of times past. Here is a simple exercise that you could repeat a thousand times and never get the same result. Shuffle your tarot deck and pull one card at random. An image on that card—a symbol, a color, or a detail—will take you back to a moment in your past. What's more, that moment will have great meaning for you now. Simply pull a card and complete this sentence: *I remember a time when* _____.

Past tense. The present is perpetually slipping away and becoming part of the past. You can see it happen with this exercise. Write about your current life in the past tense. Is there anything you want to change, now, before it's too late, and before it is permanently inscribed on the pages of history?

The words of James Barrie might inspire you: "The life of every man is a diary in which he means to write one story, and writes another; and his humblest hour is when he compares the volume as it is with what he hoped to make it."

Personal Stories

Castle of Crossed Destinies. In Italo Calvino's book *The Castle of Crossed Destinies*, an array of travelers find themselves stranded for the night in a strange castle, mysteriously stripped of their ability to speak. One of them produces a deck of tarot cards, and they all begin to share their stories, wordlessly, by choosing cards to illustrate their adventures.

Compose your own life story by selecting cards. Show them to someone else. Later, you can write in your tarot journal how you intended your story to be seen and how it was actually interpreted.

Compliments and cruelties. Write about the nicest thing anyone ever told you or the meanest thing anyone ever said about you. Find cards to represent those people, their comments, and your reaction.

Good intentions. At some time in your life, you may have intended to write a diary, to take notes, and to keep records of a monumental event or a momentous change. You may have wanted to document your baby's first year, a cross-country vacation, or a similar, life-changing event . . . until life itself got in the way, and your diary fell by the wayside.

With a tarot journal, it's never too late to re-create what might have been. Just start writing down everything you remember. Don't worry about specific dates or places; it's getting your experience down on paper that counts. The more you write, the more you will remember—and you can always turn to the cards for hints and reminders about details you may have forgotten.

Groundhog Day. In the movie *Groundhog Day,* Bill Murray is forced to relive the same day, over and over. If you could relive any day from your past, which would it be? On the other hand, which day were you glad to see end?

Sadder but Wiser

Advice for my former self. It's a common journaling technique to write letters from your current self to your former self. What do you wish you could tell your younger, less experienced self? You might also want to conduct a tarot reading on behalf of your younger self.

Crisis counseling. Think about a time in your life when you felt troubled or faced a crisis. Now imagine that you can go back in time and conduct a tarot reading on behalf of your former self. What would the cards advise? What would you recommend, as an objective tarot reader?

Slow learners. We always learn from our mistakes—but we don't always learn the "right" lesson. Some of us learn that we have rescuers, excusers, enablers, and second chances. Others learn that the excitement of crisis is its own reward for bad behavior. Pull a card or two to examine what lessons you have learned from your past.

Catch and release. Pull a single card to describe a piece of your past. Then pull a second card to describe the lesson you learned during that period. List ways in which your experience changed you. Then leave that experience in the pages of your journal, and vow not to return to it in your daily life.

My favorite mistake. We have all made mistakes. Some of us have made whoppers. What mistakes have you made that ultimately turned into something good? Maybe you married the wrong person—but you learned a lesson or two in time for your next walk down the aisle. Maybe you had an unplanned pregnancy, which led to the birth of a child you love more than life itself. Use your tarot journal to document mistakes that ultimately changed your life for the better.

Silver linings. Think back to a time when tragedy struck, everything went wrong, and you felt devastated and unsure of yourself and your future. Don't focus on mistakes you made. Rather, think about cosmic shifts that were well outside your control—like the events depicted on the Tower card. Maybe your house was hit by lightning, leveled in an earthquake, or swept away by a tidal wave. Maybe you were laid off in a sudden corporate restructuring. Maybe you were in an accident. How did you recover? How did you rise from your own ashes, like the phoenix? What new opportunities were born out of your tragedy? How is your life better now?

You done good. Make a list of at least three smart decisions you have made: going to school, for example, or changing careers, or choosing a pet. Describe the situation that led up to each decision and the factors you considered before coming to your conclusions.

The Person You Used to Be

The author and poet Joan Didion once wrote, "We are well advised to keep on nodding terms with the people we used to be, whether we find them attractive company or not. Otherwise they run up unannounced and surprise us, come hammering on the mind's door at 4 A.M. of a bad night and demand to know who deserted them, who betrayed them, who is going to make amends."

You can keep in touch with the person you used to be by memorializing him or her in your tarot journal. By writing about your past, you can reclaim pieces of your old self that may have been damaged, stolen, misplaced, or forgotten. A tarot journal can serve as a record of the person you used to be and help you reconnect with your former self.

The way we were. Pull a card to help you answer the following questions, which are based on the symbolic realms of the four suits: spiritual, emotional, intellectual, and physical.

- What did I used to believe?
- How did I used to feel?
- What did I used to know?
- What did I used to treasure?

Write about how your old beliefs, feelings, knowledge, and treasures have affected you. Did they help or did they hurt? How many of them do you still hold? Should you change them? Should you abandon them? Should you replace them? Why or why not?

Lost and found. List at least three of your favorite belongings at the age of five, ten, fifteen, or twenty (and more, if you can remember them). Reflect on the items you held during each stage of your life, revisiting your old self and your former possessions at five- or ten-year progressions.

Auld acquaintance. Pull the court cards from your tarot deck. Each one will represent someone you used to know. Who were they, and how did you know them?

You can repeat the technique with all of the wands cards, or cups, swords, or pentacles cards. You can even try it by shuffling and laying out ten cards at random.

Person, place, or thing. Alternately, look to the cards for reminders of places you used to visit, work, or live, or things you used to do.

Rewrite History

What would you do if you could turn back time? Which moment would you return to, and what would you do differently? How would the course of your life have changed?

With the tarot, you can relive—and rewrite—history. You can reconstruct your past by choosing cards to represent critical moments and decisions. Then you can experiment with different options—and different endings—simply by laying new cards on the table.

Turn back time. To try an alternate timeline at random, think of a crucial turning point in your past. Then shuffle your tarot deck and lay out three cards: one for the period that led up to that point, one for the moment of decision, and a third card for the consequences of that decision. Finally, lay a fourth card. Imagine that it represents an alternate course of events. How might your life have changed? Write about it in your journal.

The road not taken. According to the theory of quantum physics, all possibilities are realities somewhere. While you eliminate certain paths simply by choosing one option over another, you may have parallel selves in parallel universes who choose the roads you didn't take.

Think about the choices you opted not to take and the paths you didn't follow. What would have happened in your life if you had made a different choice . . . married a different person, accepted a different job, had a child, or stayed childless? Then write your life story as your parallel self. If you now find yourself as a social studies teacher in Wisconsin, you could travel back in time and write about what might have been:

> I married Bob in 1992. We moved to New York City and I found a job in public relations. I worked in a towering skyscraper for six years. I was promoted several times, but I was never quite comfortable with the politics of corporate life. Finally, I quit my job and moved upstate, where I became a potter and started selling my creations at craft shows throughout New England.

Alternate endings. Deena Metzger, the author of *Writing for Your Life,* describes a technique she terms "creating a usable history." If you don't like the story of your life, you can use your tarot journal to create a new life story for yourself—and change the outcome of an unhappy or unfortunate experience. Was your mother cold and unfeeling? Write about the caregiver you wish you had—a warm and nurturing parent who baked you cookies and read you bedtime stories. Were you an unpopular teenager? In your journal, you can describe your days as the head cheerleader and homecoming queen. Simply write your life story as you would have liked it to read in the first place.

While the process of rewriting history might not change reality, it will change your attitude. As Willa Cather said, "Some memories are realities, and are better than anything that can ever happen to one again."

6
What Lies Before You

Turn up the sixth card; place it on the side that the Significator is facing, and say: This is before him. It shews the influence that is coming into action and will operate in the near future.

—ARTHUR EDWARD WAITE,
The Pictorial Key to the Tarot (1910)

How to Use Your Tarot Journal to Design Your Future

We all want to know what will happen next. We watch the weather forecast on the evening news. We listen for traffic reports on the radio. We read our horoscopes in the daily paper.

And we read tarot cards.

While you can't control the weather and you can't always avoid a rush-hour traffic jam, you can use tarot cards to take control of your destiny. With the cards and your journal in hand, you can do more than simply wait for the future to unfold: you can create it. What's more, the only magic wand you will need is your pen.

Seal the Deal

Ordinary tarot readings can often inspire us with good news about the future, encourage us to continue on a path, or caution us to make changes. If you don't take notes in your tarot journal, however, the cards will probably fade from memory, like the dream you forget by the time you drink your first morning cup of coffee.

If you want to seal a reading and imbue it with power, write it down. When you record your readings in your tarot journal, you give physical substance and shape to ideas and concepts—simply by representing them in the form of letters and words.

By keeping a record of your tarot readings, you will also start a chain of events in motion. You will discover new ways to express the cards' messages in your daily life. You can start to manifest the messages of the cards and generate follow-through in the world around you.

Make Plans

You can use your tarot journal as a planning guide. Maya Angelou once said, "Each of us has the right and the responsibility to assess the roads which lie ahead and those over which we have traveled, and if the future road looms ominous or unpromising, and the roads back uninviting, then we need to gather our resolve and, carrying only the necessary baggage, step off that road into another direction."

Start planning for your future by assessing your present. Look through your tarot deck until you see a card that depicts your current spiritual, emotional, intellectual, or physical state. How did you get here? Then find a second card to represent the goal you want to achieve. How will you reach it? Try this three-step process:

1: Set goals. Summarize your goal in a single sentence. *I will sell my company and move to a house in the country.*

2: List milestones. List the milestones you will need to reach—with a time frame, if possible.

> *I need to boost sales by 42 percent within the next six months.*
>
> *I need to write a marketing plan by June 30.*
>
> *I need to hire an additional salesperson in the next two weeks.*
>
> *I need to write a business plan by August 31.*
>
> *By the time I start writing the business plan, I need to find a broker to handle the sale of the company.*
>
> *I will sell the company and move into a new house by New Year's Eve.*

3: Chart your progress. Leave space in your tarot journal to note the actions you take, the results you attain, and your steady progress toward your goal.

Brainstorm

Mark McElroy offers a wide range of brainstorming techniques in his book *Putting the Tarot to Work.* One is to flip quickly through all of the cards in the Major Arcana—the Fool through the World—and glean one idea from each, as if each character were offering you his or her own take on your situation. Need advice? Ask each archetype what you should do. Need a critique? Gather your tarot-card focus group together and start gathering opinions. Need information? Ask your tarot-card counselors what they know.

Back to the Future

In the *Back to the Future* movie trilogy, young Marty McFly travels back and forth through time, watching history unfold and making adjustments in an effort to keep events on course.

You can use your tarot deck like a time machine, too. By picturing yourself in the future, you can make adjustments to ensure that your history unfolds as you like.

Creative visualization. "To bring anything into your life, imagine that it's already there," Richard Bach said—and tarot cards are a great source of visual inspiration and thoughtful suggestions.

Start simply by envisioning yourself a month from now, a year from now, or ten years from now. Where will you live? Where will you work? Who will you be with? Visualize your ideal partner, your ideal home, your ideal job, and your ideal self. Be as detailed as you can—and look for specific cards to represent each option. What will you look like? How will you feel? What will you do with your time? Find tarot cards to suit all of your needs and desires.

Record your choices in your tarot journal, along with the reasons you used to make each decision.

Flash forward. Sit down and imagine that you can do a reading for your future self. What advice do the cards have for the person you will become? What advice do you have for the person you want to become? What do you want to remember as you move toward your goals?

A word to the wise. Here's a real time-warp technique: project yourself into the future and allow your future self to do a reading for your present self. Read the cards as someone who has already attained the goals you have in mind. See if that changes your perspective. It will be possible, if you believe as T. S. Eliot did, that:

Time present and time past
Are both perhaps present in time future,
And time future contained in time past.

Future tense. Write a letter to your future self and a letter from your future self. Remind your future self what you presently think about your life and how you would like your life to change.

Special Requests

Pencil it in. It's astounding how often the universe will respond to your clearly stated request—especially if it's in writing. "The very act of seeking sets something in motion to meet us," said Jean Shinoda Bolen. "Something in the universe or in the unconscious responds as if to an invitation."

The act of entering your hopes and dreams into your journal will help you clarify them in your mind, picture the results, and prepare for the possibilities. What's more, unless you carve them in stone, you can amend them if you change your mind.

Spell It Out

In ancient times, most people couldn't read or write, and those who could were thought to possess a certain kind of magic power. After all, they had the power to transcribe spoken words, and transform thoughts into reality.

You still have the power to cast spells—even in the most magical sense of the word—by spelling out your fondest hopes and dreams in the pages of your tarot journal. Simply record your hopes, dreams, wishes, and goals in as much detail as you can possibly muster.

7
Your Self

The seventh card of the operation signifies himself—that is, the Significator—whether person or thing—and shews its position or attitude in the circumstances.

—ARTHUR EDWARD WAITE,
The Pictorial Key to the Tarot (1910)

Who Do You Think You Are?

The avant-garde novelist Anaïs Nin is best known for documenting her own life in a series of published diaries. As she recorded her experiences over several decades, she came to one powerful conclusion.

"We don't see things as they are," she wrote, "we see things as we are."

How do you see yourself? What are your strengths and your weaknesses? How do you express your spiritual beliefs, your emotions, your thoughts, and your values? And as a result, how do you see the world?

Your tarot journal can lead you through a process of self-assessment and self-development. As you see and express yourself more clearly, your view of the world could change, too.

Worlds of Experience

In tarot, the four realms of everyday experience are represented by the four suits of the Minor Arcana. Wands represent your spiritual life, cups depict your emotional affairs, swords conceptualize your intellectual ideals, and pentacles embody your physical existence.

You can use your tarot journal to analyze those four realms of your experience, both separately and as a whole. You can see where most of your focus lies, where your experiences overlap, and where you have room to grow and change.

Your Spiritual Self

The fiery wands cards, which usually picture freshly cut branches from leafy trees, represent the world of spiritual existence. They symbolize inspirations and drives, passions, and primal quests.

Think of the wands cards as you work with the following journal prompts:

Spiritually, I believe _____.

Spiritually, I feel _____.

Spiritually, I think _____.

Spiritually, I am _____.

Spiritually, I value _____.

Spiritually, I have _____.

Spiritually, I need _____.

Spiritually, I would like to _____.

Spiritually, I am becoming more _____.

Spiritually, I secretly_____.

Spiritually, I express myself by _____.

My greatest spiritual skill is _____.

My greatest spiritual weakness is _____.

The card that best depicts my spiritual life is _____.

Your Emotional Self

The watery cups cards usually picture goblets and chalices filled with water or wine, as well as a wide range of individuals in emotional situations. The cups cards symbolize the world of attitudes, feelings, and relationships with others.

Think of the cups cards as you work with the following journal prompts:

Emotionally, I believe _____.

Emotionally, I feel _____.

Emotionally, I think _____.

Emotionally, I am _____.

Emotionally, I value _____.

Emotionally, I have _____.

Emotionally, I need _____.

Emotionally, I would like to _____.

Emotionally, I am becoming more _____.

Emotionally, I secretly _____.

Emotionally, I express myself by _____.

My greatest emotional skill is _____.

My greatest emotional weakness is _____.

The card that best depicts my emotional life is _____.

Your Intellectual Self

The airy swords cards usually picture sharpened swords, which represent the heady world of the intellect. Swords symbolize the airy issues of thought and communication, as well as the words we use to defend ourselves and attack those with whom we disagree.

Think of the swords cards as you work with the following journal prompts:

> Intellectually, I believe _____.
>
> Intellectually, I feel _____.
>
> Intellectually, I think _____.
>
> Intellectually, I am _____.
>
> Intellectually, I value _____.
>
> Intellectually, I have _____.
>
> Intellectually, I need _____.
>
> Intellectually, I would like to _____.
>
> Intellectually, I am becoming more _____.
>
> Intellectually, I secretly_____.
>
> Intellectually, I express myself by _____.
>
> My greatest intellectual strength is _____.
>
> My greatest intellectual weakness is _____.
>
> The card that best depicts my intellectual life is _____.

Your Physical Self

The earthy pentacles cards usually depict coins, which represent the tangible realities of physical life. Pentacles represent the things we can touch, the things we can feel, and the things we treasure—both material and spiritual.

Think of the pentacles cards as you work with the following journal prompts:

Physically, I believe _____.

Physically, I feel _____.

Physically, I think _____.

Physically, I am _____.

Physically, I value _____.

Physically, I have _____.

Physically, I need _____.

Physically, I would like to _____.

Physically, I am becoming more _____.

Physically, I secretly_____.

Physically, I express myself by _____.

My greatest physical strength is _____.

My greatest physical weakness is _____.

The card that best depicts my physical life is _____.

Birth Cards and Year Cards

In addition to self-assessment through journaling, you can learn more about yourself by studying your birth card and year cards.

Both are typically derived from simple numerology. One common way to find your birth card is to add the numbers of your birth date together, like this: M+M+D+D+Y+Y+Y+Y.

Take Emily, for example, who was born on October 24, 1992. To find her birth card, Emily would add the numbers of her birth month (10), birthday (24), and birth year (1992). The numbers would look like this: 1+0+2+4+1+9+9+2. (That's 10-24-1992.)

The sum should be a number between 1 and 21, which will correspond to one of the Major Arcana cards. In Emily's case, however, the end result is 28.

If, like Emily, your result is more than 21, add those two numbers together. Emily would add 2+8, and get 10. That means her birth card is card number ten, the Wheel of Fortune.

That also means that she is one of the lucky people who actually get more than one birth card. She can add the 1+0 for a second card, which would be card number one, the Magician.

Your birth card will be your birth card for as long as you live. However, you might also discover that other Major Arcana cards seem to reflect a predominant theme for every year of your life.

You do, in fact, get a new year card every time your birthday rolls around. Simply use the same mathematical formula to determine which card will come into play as you grow a year older. When Emily turns forty, for example, on October 24, 2032, she can determine her year card by adding 1+0+2+4+2+0+3+2. She'll get 14: the Temperance card.

In a way, knowing your birth card and year cards is kind of like knowing your astrological sun sign. You will obviously share your birth card and year cards with many other people—there are only twenty-one cards to go around. But you will also be able to identify some personality traits and characteristics that you couldn't otherwise explain. If you are a born Magician, for example, raised in a family of decidedly non-magical personalities like Hermits and Hanged Men, you might suddenly understand why you didn't fit in with the rest of your relatives. And if your life suddenly seems to be disrupted during a Tower year, you can make any attitude adjustments you need—and know that a Star year is coming up next.

To learn more about the attributes associated with every Major Arcana card, consult a standard tarot textbook, such as Anthony Louis's *Tarot Plain and Simple* or Teresa Michelsen's *Complete Tarot Reader*.

Facets of the Jewel

Psychologists often say that every symbol and image in a dream is an aspect of the dreamer's personality. The rabid dog that hounds you in your midnight hours might actually represent the wild animal side of your own human nature. The flower garden of your dreams—lush, green, and blossoming with color—might also symbolize your desire to cultivate your own creative talents.

The same holds true when it comes to the tarot deck. Every card in a seventy-eight-card deck represents one aspect of your personality. The Five of Wands might represent your playful, adolescent self. The Three of Cups might depict your role as a friend and confidant to others.

You can use the cards to come to terms with the many facets and sides of your personality, simply by choosing the ones that most accurately depict the traits that you recognize—and also by determining how the less familiar cards fit into your psychological makeup.

Start by working with the cards that suit you best. Write about them in your journal: describe how you identify with them, why you identify with them, and why you value the traits and characteristics they represent. (If you don't value them, write about how they came to be part of your personality, and what you plan to do with them in the future.)

As time goes on, you can also write about the cards that don't seem to be an especially strong part of your makeup.

Role Play

You can develop a stronger sense of self—and integrate your various subpersonalities better—by using the tarot as the basis for some easy role-playing games. Simply choose to live as a tarot card, just for a day.

Select any card, either face up or face down, and study the character on the card. Notice how he or she stands, or sits, and try to stand, sit, and move as you imagine that character would.

Pay attention to how the figure is dressed: wear a similar outfit, if you can, or simply choose clothes with the same colors or patterns.

Picture what he or she might do for fun, and see if you can't fit a similar activity into your schedule. Yes, the King of Pentacles probably does enjoy bowling: check to see if there's an open lane in your neighborhood bowling alley tonight. Judgement blows a horn; you might want to pick up a musical instrument, too. If there are horse-drawn carriages for rent in your area, it might be time for you to take a little Chariot ride. Use your imagination.

To fully imbue yourself with the essence of a tarot card, you can even try to eat a meal that the characters in each card would enjoy. For menu ideas, consult *The Epicurean Tarot,* a collection of recipe cards based on the tarot.

When you are through living out the archetype of a tarot card, be sure to record your experiences in your tarot journal.

Masks of Personality

Actors in ancient Greek dramas relied on exaggerated costumes and masks to express the defining characteristics of their roles, as well as to enlarge movements and gestures that would otherwise be difficult for their audiences to discern.

If you sometimes worry that your actions are overlooked, or the full range of your emotions isn't being fully expressed, you can play with a similar technique. Simply rehearse a range of scenes and acts from your real life as if you were an actor on a stage—and use tarot cards as your mask. Hold the card of your choice in front of your face, and pretend you are the character in that card.

If you are playing the role of Temperance, for example, you might want to portray her in your most graceful manner, with perfect posture and an evenly modulated speaking voice. If you are the Four of Swords, you might want to move to the couch and say your lines while you lie flat on your back.

Afterward, write about it in your tarot journal, and see how much of your role-playing carries over into your everyday life.

8
Your House

The eighth card signifies his house, that is, his environment and the tendencies at work therein which have an effect on the matter—for instance, his position in life, the influence of immediate friends, and so forth.

—ARTHUR EDWARD WAITE,
The Pictorial Key to the Tarot (1910)

Journaling about Family and Friends

In *Welcome to the Great Mysterious*, author Lorna Landvik tells the story of Geneva Jordan, a forty-something Broadway star who stumbles across an old family scrapbook. As a child, Geneva and her twin sister had filled the scrapbook with existential questions. "What is true love?" they asked. "What is the meaning of life?" Each night, as the children slept, Geneva's parents and grandparents would quietly take turns writing answers to the children's questions.

Years later, as Geneva re-read their words, she found herself reconnecting with people she had loved and lost—and rediscovering her former self.

You can use your tarot journal to help you rebuild relationships, reconcile old grievances, and reconnect with your family and friends—even if you can't connect in real life.

The Royal Family

The tarot deck's four sets of court cards represent four idealized families: father, mother, brother, and sister. Choose the court card family that most closely represents your family. Wands would indicate a family that is spiritually strong, or structured around a shared spirituality. Cups court cards might symbolize a family that is emotional. Swords court cards could represent a family that is intellectually strong, with values, intellect, and communication. Pentacles probably would indicate a family that values physical agility and expression.

Now use a mix of court cards, along with relevant Major and Minor Arcana cards, to more accurately depict the strengths and weaknesses of your individual family members. If your mother reminds you of the Queen of Cups, for example, with just a hint of the Page of Swords or the Two of Wands, use all three cards in combination to represent her—and explain the reason for your selections in your journal.

Forget Me Not

Sadly, it's a fact of life that as you grow older, your connection to the past will fade. As the years pass, you will inevitably begin to lose the people you have always known—like your grandparents, your aunts and uncles, and old family friends.

No matter what happens, however, you can keep them alive in the pages of your tarot journal.

Family history. Write down everything about your family history that you know to be a fact. Check with your other family members for their versions of the story.

If you like, you can turn to the cards to fill in the missing pieces. How was grandma feeling when she came over on the ship from the old country? Was she dancing with her fellow travelers in the Three of Cups? Or did she seem more like the solitary wanderer in the Eight of Cups?

Individual histories. Use the cards to reconstruct the life story of someone close to you—your mother, father, husband, or wife. Compare your own tarot-based timeline to theirs. You may discover intriguing new ways in which your paths paralleled, crossed, or parted ways with each other.

Family reunion. Make a list of all the people you love and know well, and the people you interact with on a regular basis. They can include your family members—parents, grandparents, aunts and uncles, brothers and sisters, spouse, and children—as well as your classmates, friends, neighbors, and coworkers. Which tarot card reminds you of each one? Why?

Skeletons in the closet. What secrets did your family guard from outsiders? What secrets did your family members keep from each other? What secrets did you only understand once you had reached adulthood? Use tarot cards to bring your family's secrets out of the shadows and into the pages of your journal.

Karmic connections. Some say you can choose your friends, but you can't choose your relatives. On a spiritual level, however, some people believe that we do choose the families we are born into. Some people believe that our souls agree to be born into a certain place and time to live with a predetermined set of parents, brothers, and sisters, and to learn from the experience.

Whether or not you accept that premise, try it in your tarot journal. Pull one card from your tarot deck, at random, for information about why you might have chosen the people in your life. The card will trigger your memory and help you recognize the lessons you have learned from your family, the visions you share, and the gifts you have received from your relationships.

What did your father have to teach you? What gifts did your mother give you? What have you learned from your grandparents, aunts, and uncles? You can pull a card for every person who has played a significant role in your life—and start to write about how their presence has helped you understand the world and yourself.

Keep in touch. Start a journal to share with a friend or family member. Take turns writing in it, like Geneva Jordan's family did in *Welcome to the Great Mysterious.* When you want to exchange it, simply leave it on the table, on a living room chair, or on each other's pillows. If you live miles apart, mail it back and forth. A shared journal is more fun than sending letters, and when you have filled its pages you will have a piece of family history to treasure forever. You can even plan to leave it to your children or grandchildren.

See and be seen. How do your friends and family members see you? Write about yourself from any other person's point of view—maybe your brother, your sister, or your great-aunt. You could even pull a tarot card from the deck, and imagine that you are a character in the card. Look at yourself from that character's vantage point. How would you describe the person you see?

By writing about your life from someone else's perspective, you can start to see yourself as others see you. You might even start to understand their point of view.

Unsent letters. Use your journal to write a letter to someone who affected you strongly as a child. You might want to challenge them or question them about something they said or did to you. You might also want to thank them or praise them for their handling of a certain situation. If you have any unfinished business with the person, address it in your letter.

Familiar strangers. Experienced tarot readers often notice a strange phenomenon: when they read cards for other people, they inevitably find that the cards seem to reflect issues and events that are prominent in their own lives. Test the phenomenon for yourself. Find a place where you can read for people you don't know. Offer to read for strangers in a coffee shop, for example, or at a party. If you aren't comfortable reading for others, choose a name at random from an article in the newspaper—before you have read it.

Do you notice any parallels between your life and those for whom you read? What issues seem to overlap? What messages do the cards hold for you? Record them in your tarot journal.

9
Your Hopes and Fears

The ninth card gives his hopes or fears in the matter.

—ARTHUR EDWARD WAITE,
The Pictorial Key to the Tarot (1910)

Plumbing the Depths and Climbing New Heights

In a Celtic Cross tarot reading, one card represents both hopes and fears. How can a single card symbolize two separate issues? Because hope and fear are inextricably linked. They are two sides of the same coin—or pentacle, if you will.

How often have you wished for something big—a new car, a new job, a new relationship—but held off, just a bit, for fear that you might actually get what you wish for? After all, a new car usually comes with a hefty price tag. A new job involves writing résumés, cover letters, scouring the want ads, and dressing up for interviews. And a new relationship takes time, energy, and commitment. Sometimes, it's just easier to stay home and watch TV.

Your tarot journal is the perfect place for you to explore your most fervent desires and your deepest, darkest fears, before you take steps to materialize them in the real world.

Hope Springs Eternal

Hopes are easy to write about. We all have high hopes for the future, as well as innumerable hopes for the next day, the next week, or the next month. In fact, your challenge in a tarot journal may be to limit the number of things you merely hope for, and focus on turning those hopes into reality.

In the meantime, however, you can start listing some of those hopes.

Wish list. Make a list of all the things you hope will come true for you in the next year. Then pull a card to get advice about each item on the list. Should you pursue it? If so, how?

Success stories. Make a list of things you have hoped for in the past and achieved. How did you attain each one? Do you see any patterns? Do you see any advice for achieving your current hopes?

Secret wishes. Pull a card to represent a hope you haven't yet recognized or thought about consciously. What do you want?

Why ask why? Think of something you have hoped for for some time that hasn't yet come about. Ask yourself why—not once or twice, but repeatedly—until you run out of answers.

> *What are your hopes? Why?*
>
> *Why haven't you attained those hopes?*
>
> *Why haven't you reached your goals?*
>
> *What will change in your life if you reach your goals?*
>
> *What steps must you take to achieve them?*

Fear Factors

"Sometimes," Eleanor Roosevelt said, "you must do the things you think you cannot do." You can test that theory in your tarot journal. Before you face your fears in real life, you can confront them on paper.

Boo! Pull a card at random from the deck. Some symbol or image on the card will represent one of your fears. What is it? Write about it, stream-of-consciousness style.

Check the lineup. Which card in the tarot deck seems to illustrate your fear? Which card illustrates the way you handle your fear? Describe the connections in your journal.

The origin of the species. Think about a fear you have experienced for a long time—a fear of heights, for example, or snakes, or public speaking. Which card illustrates the origin of your fear? A symbol or an image may suddenly reveal what you need to know.

Worst-case scenarios. Assume, for a moment, you have pulled a card that represents your deepest, darkest fear. Take time to explore it in your journal. Use a simple question-and-answer technique to determine the worst-case scenarios that are at the heart of your fears, and follow each one to its logical conclusion.

It might get gruesome; after all, this is your "fears" section. But don't be afraid to keep going. By examining your fears and following each one to its logical conclusion, you could start to resolve issues that otherwise lie just underneath the surface, worrying and gnawing at you. Some of your fears could even start to resolve themselves. At the very least, you'll be able to name and describe your fears—and there's something to be said for knowing your enemy.

Take the Death card, for example.

Q: *What frightens you most about the Death card?*
A: *It reminds me that I could die. I could be in a car accident or something.*

Q: *In that situation, what would be the worst-case scenario?*
A: *I would be dead.*

Q: *What would happen then?*
A: *Well, personally, I think I would be okay, because I believe in an afterlife.*

Q: *So what worries you about dying? What's the worst-case scenario?*
A: *My children would lose their mother.*

Q: *What would happen to them?*
A: *Their father would raise them.*

Q: *In that situation, what would be the worst-case scenario?*
A: *In the worst-case scenario, he might die, too.*

Q: *What if you both were killed? What would happen then?*
A: *My sister and her husband would raise my children. Actually, I think that's the logical conclusion I need to reach. If I were dead, my children would be motherless, but I guess that's beyond my control. I've made sure they would still have loving adults to step in and raise them. I suppose I can live with that.*

Meet face to face. Choose a card from the tarot deck to represent one of your fears. Then use your journal to have a written conversation with that card. Imagine, for example, that you are afraid of public speaking, and that you have chosen the confident, outspoken King of Wands to symbolize your fear.

Q: *Why am I afraid of you?*
A: *Because I represent power and authority.*

Q: *I want power and authority.*
A: *No, you don't. Because you don't want the responsibility that goes along with it.*

Q: *What do you mean? I'm a responsible person. In fact, I feel a little insulted.*

A: *When you take on the role of authority, you're going to have to take a stand on certain issues. And once you take a stand, you won't be universally liked. You're going to ruffle some feathers. Right now, it's more important for you to be liked than to be respected.*

Unreasonable fears. Make a list of all of your "unreasonable" fears—a fear of clowns, for example, or mountain climbing or red-headed men named Chuck. How did you develop your un-reasonable fears? Where did they come from? Why do you hold on to them? What purpose do they serve in your life? Explore them. You might discover that you have perfectly reasonable explanations for your fears—as well as an array of coping methods to ease their burden.

10
What Will Come

The tenth is what will come, the final result, the culmination which is brought about by the influences shewn by the other cards that have been turned up in the divination.

It is on this card that the Diviner should especially concentrate his intuitive faculties and his memory in respect of the official divinatory meanings attached thereto. It should embody whatsoever you may have divined from the other cards on the table, including the Significator itself and concerning him or it, not excepting such lights upon higher significance as might fall like sparks from heaven if the card which serves for the oracle, the card for reading, should happen to be a Trump Major.

—ARTHUR EDWARD WAITE,
The Pictorial Key to the Tarot (1910)

Foretelling the Future

Can tarot cards tell the future?

Many of today's tarot readers would probably bristle at the question. Tarot cards, of course, have a reputation as a fortunetelling device. For centuries, the cards have been purveyed by mystics, fortunetellers, gypsies, and seers. Many people still think of the tarot primarily in conjunction with divination and fortunetelling—at best, a harmless pastime, and at worst, a tool for charlatans, frauds, con artists, and swindlers.

In the last few decades, however, the tarot has been reclaimed by a new generation of readers, and the cards are no longer strictly limited to divination. Tarot cards are widely used as an aid to meditation, reflection, self-examination, and self-development. Writers, artists, and storytellers use them as inspiration for their creative efforts. Psychiatrists, psychologists, and counselors use the cards like a sophisticated deck of Rorschach blots, prompting their clients to look into their own life stories to make sense of their own past, present, and future.

The tarot, its proponents would argue, is much more than a parlor game for giddy school girls and bored housewives. The tarot, they would tell you, is a psychological tool, ideally suited to aid us in the quest for understanding and self-development. The tarot is also a useful device for unleashing creativity and unblocking communication.

But every now and then, a parlor game can be a lot of fun. For most of us, it can be wildly entertaining to read the cards with an eye to the future and try to predict when a tall, dark stranger will cross your path.

Even when the cards are read just for fun, a naysayer might point out that most "fortunetellers" overstate their abilities. Obviously, tarot cards can depict the road you have taken, the path you are on, and your most likely destination . . . But then again, it doesn't take a lot of skill to see where most people are headed. Much of the work that is touted as fortunetelling is merely common sense.

Many experts, including famed psychiatrist Carl Jung, believe that the tarot taps into the collective unconscious—the underlying bond of energy, emotion, and shared experience that unites us all.

Others believe that users are simply drawn instinctively to the symbols in each card that have the most meaning and significance for them.

Every now and then, however, tarot readers seem to pick up on future developments, with very little to go on—either from the cards or from the observations they make about a client.

Does the tarot really have the power to predict the future?

No. But people do. So while no one can honestly say that tarot cards are psychic, you might be.

Fortunetelling and the Tarot

Psychic ability isn't talked about much—even among tarot readers, who depend on their psychic gifts every day. Maybe it's the word itself. Some people think the term "psychic" connotes sham artists, con games, and gimmicks. It might make us think of spooky-looking women who crack open bloody eggs and mutter dark-sounding curses, all to trick the desperate and the gullible out of their life savings.

That hardly describes most of the tarot readers in the real world, who spend most of their time as mild-mannered accountants, beauticians, doctors, dentists, administrative assistants, and business owners . . . in short, as ordinary people.

Even tarot readers who make a living with their psychic skills tend to call themselves "intuitive" rather than psychic. For one thing, the "intuitive" label takes tarot out of the realm of gypsy wagons and storefronts with neon signs. It's kinder, gentler, and far more down-to-earth. What's more, it's a term that's based in our scientific understanding of the conscious and unconscious mind. It's easy to explain that we can make a few observations about another person or a situation, mix the information up a bit in our subconscious, and come up with an accurate analysis via the cards. By calling our talent intuitive, we can easily reassure ourselves—and any skeptics and disbelievers—that the cards operate according to logical, rational rules.

However, intuition simply doesn't explain how tarot readers can glean so many personal details about other people just from looking at a few pieces of cardboard. There are too many times when the information that comes up in a tarot reading can't be written off as merely a good guess.

There's something else to consider, too. When we call our gifts intuitive, we diminish them. We make them smaller. We claim them as our own creations, and we trace their origin back to our inner-most selves, rather than accepting our psychic talent as a gift from a power greater than ourselves. And, in many ways, we limit our use of the tarot. A tarot reader who is open to receiving information psychically can offer much more than one who wants to adhere to the here and now. And tarot readers who admit that some of their insight comes from a source outside of themselves won't feel afraid, ashamed, or compelled to account for that information. They can freely offer whatever knowledge or insight they glean from the cards without embarrassment or apology.

No matter what psychic gifts they have, most people find that working with a psychic tool like the tarot will help them develop and refine their talents. But what many people don't realize is that tarot cards are also handy for people who are naturally very psychic. Some are so sensitive that they block out every impression, simply to get through a normal day. For them, tarot cards can be just as useful as they are for those with little natural ability. They can use the cards to filter their psychic stimuli, just as others use the cards to magnify and enhance their skills.

Granted, you don't need to be psychic to use the tarot—but it doesn't hurt. Most experts even say that using tools like the tarot can help you develop your innate psychic gifts.

Types of Psychic Ability

There are several widely recognized types of psychic ability, all of which could play a role in your tarot reading and journaling practice.

Telepathy. Telepathy is the ability to send and receive mental images. During a tarot reading with another person, you may pick up on unspoken thoughts and feelings. You might find yourself drawn to one card or one image that reflects the main issue or concern.

Don't be afraid to let those unspoken signals guide your reading. In fact, try to verbalize those messages, so you can get confirmation from the other person.

Be sure to write down your psychic impressions in your tarot journal. As you do, let your imagination run wild. Don't block out any impressions, and don't regard any information you receive as too silly or too nonsensical to be considered. Rather, accept coincidences and look for synchronicity.

When you give yourself permission to let go, you will probably be surprised by your psychic accuracy.

Clairvoyance is the ability to see the future or gain an awareness of another time and place. The information isn't always visual, however. Most often, clairvoyance is expressed as a sudden flash of insight or understanding that springs suddenly into one's consciousness.

If you would like to develop your clairvoyant skills, look at a single tarot card as if you were looking at a photo in a newspaper. Breathe deeply, let your focus relax, and simply gaze at the image. You might see one feature of the card gain new prominence. It might seem to shimmer, shift, or rise up and become three-dimensional. Stay calm, continue to hold the card, and watch what happens. Record any impressions you have. As you feel more confident, you can even do the same exercise with design-based pip cards, like those in the *Marseille Tarot* or an ordinary deck of playing cards.

You might also like to experiment with conducting tarot readings only in your mind's eye. Lay out a standard tarot card spread, but keep all of the cards face down. Don't turn them over; simply imagine what each card might be and read the cards as if you could see them face up. Record your reading in your tarot journal without looking at the front of the cards. Afterward, check your work. How clear were your impressions? How accurate was your reading?

Clairaudience is the ability to "hear" messages from the metaphysical or spirit world. Sometimes clairaudience comes in the form of a voice or a sound that originates outside the listener. People with clairaudient experiences might hear an urgent shout of warning, for example, or footsteps in an empty house, or music that seems to come out of nowhere. More common, however, is the clairaudient who describes a quiet voice inside his or her head.

A clairaudient experience is not the same as a psychotic episode. In fact, it is common to experience clairaudience during tarot readings. As you look at a tarot card, you may hear a word or a phrase inside your head. If you try to ignore it, you will probably hear it again and again, until you acknowledge it.

If you are reading the cards for someone else, don't be afraid or embarrassed to say things that seem to make no sense. They may know exactly what you mean. And if you have a clairaudient experience while you are reading the cards for yourself, write it down in your tarot journal, and see if it makes sense once events have had time to unfold.

Psychometry is the ability to receive information through touch. Some psychics can get a mental picture or personality clues simply by holding an object that belongs to someone else.

If you want to enhance your own skills at psychometry, shuffle your tarot deck and fan the cards out, face down. Slowly pass your hand over the cards. Do some seem to radiate heat? Do some feel cold? Does your hand seem to tingle as it passes over the cards? Those may be the cards that have special significance for you.

Just for fun, you might also want to have a friend choose three Major Arcana cards from the deck and put each one in a sealed envelope. Without knowing which cards are inside, hold each envelope in your hands, and then write down your impressions.

Precognition and prediction both describe the ability to foretell the future. To test your precognitive ability, just shuffle a tarot deck, face down. Before you turn each card in the deck face up, guess whether it is from the Major Arcana or the Minor Arcana. If you are right, you get to keep the card. If you are wrong, put it in a discard pile. Give yourself a pat on the back for every card you call correctly.

You might also like to try an exercise that's pure visualization. First, picture yourself shuffling your favorite tarot deck. Then imagine yourself cutting the cards. Finally, envision yourself turning over the top three cards. Which ones are they? Write them down. To check your work, shuffle and cut your deck for real, and lay out a classic Celtic Cross. Do those same three cards show up anywhere in your reading?

To develop your skills at prediction, practice. Start by making predictions based on stories from the daily news; how will each story play out? What will happen to the newsmakers tomorrow or next week or next month?

Alternately, you could write down ten or twenty questions in your tarot journal, and predict the answers. Date each one, and check your accuracy later.

One word of caution: Be wary of making predictions about illnesses, accidents, or events of a tragic nature. The tarot speaks the language of symbols and metaphor. The cards are not particularly good at predicting physical death, disease, or destruction.

Prediction may be the most difficult skill you will attempt to develop as a tarot reader. It's common to discover, as you review old readings in your journal, that the cards were accurate—but your predictions were wildly off base. When you review your entries, you will often see where your interpretation went astray. Maybe it was in the way you phrased the questions; you might have been unclear or failed to suggest a time frame for the answer. You might even have based your predictions on your own expectations, rather than what the cards said.

It's also important to remember that the future is never set in stone. While tarot cards can suggest the most likely outcome of someone's current path, the future is not predetermined. The decisions people make—perhaps as the result of a tarot reading—can and will affect their end results.

As Richard Bach once said, "You're always free to change your mind and choose a different future."

Guidelines for Psychic Development

Before you begin any work with the tarot or with psychic development, you might want to keep a few ground rules in mind:

Cheer up. Make sure you feel enthusiastic, optimistic, and energized before you sit down to practice your psychic skills.

Don't do any psychic work if you're tired, sick, depressed, or out of sorts. That's because "like attracts like"—and if you're in a funk, a psychic practice session probably won't be enough to pull you out of it. You might even compound the problem, because any number of sad, lonely spirits might decide to drop by and commiserate with you.

Stay sober. Don't practice your psychic gifts while you're under the influence of alcohol or drugs. When you get behind the wheel of psychic development, you will be operating heavy machinery—and a DUI on the metaphysical highway could have cosmic consequences.

Be alert. Don't feel pressured to add psychic development to a long list of "to do's." These days, many people are chronically sleep-deprived, which can have the same effect on psychic ability as illness, drugs, and drinking. You might find you are as psychic as you need to be already—but you are also too tired to act on it. Maybe all you really need is a nap.

Ground yourself. Odd as it sounds, you need to be grounded physically before you can take off spiritually. So once you have caught up on your sleep, go for a brisk walk. Fill your lungs with fresh air. If you can see open sky or be near water, so much the better. If you really want to rejuvenate your spirit, indulge your senses: Listen to music. Visit a museum or an art gallery. Buy some new incense, a scented candle, or perfume. Take a long bath or shower. Eat something. For both practical and symbolic reasons, you should also drink plenty of water. If you're very metaphysical, you might think of it as increasing your receptivity. If you're more practical, you might just realize that any concentrated effort—even spiritual work—can be both psychically and physically draining.

Wear protection. Remember to shield yourself psychically. Most people don't head for the beach without sun block and a T-shirt. You shouldn't scamper unprotected into the spirit world, either. If you don't yet have a shielding routine, start with the basics. Sit up straight and put both feet on the floor, so you are well-grounded in every sense of the word. Breathe slowly and deeply. Close your eyes and visualize a beam of white light coming down from the sky above you, encasing you in a protective, warm embrace. Announce your intentions in the form of a prayer or a meditation, and ask for support. You might want to have the Temperance card nearby to represent your guardian angel or spirit guide.

Come back to the real world. When your psychic session concludes, offer thanks for the insight and information you received, and then close up shop for the day. While you never need to let your psychic shield down, you can let it slip from your conscious awareness—at least until the next time you come to the tarot reader's table.

Documenting Your Success

If you want to use your tarot journal to develop your intuition and hone your psychic ability, keep a comprehensive record of your tarot readings. Note the cards that appear, along with their positions and significance.

Write down all of your impressions about the cards—especially if your insights seem wildly out of line. Also, keep a record of any unanswered questions that crop up during your readings. Leave space so you can review your records as events unfold. As time passes, you can refer back to your journal for additional insights into events as they occur and as they are resolved.

Before long, the notes in your tarot journal will help you learn what personal meaning the cards have for you. If you think of a new romance every time you see the Two of Wands—and that proves to be the case in your own experience—you will bring that non-standard interpretation to the table every time you sit down to read the cards.

With time, you will probably be surprised to discover how intuitive you are—and your tarot journal will serve to confirm your wisdom and insight.

APPENDIX I

Writing Prompts

If you are looking for something to write about in your journal, try one of the following prompts.

Choose any prompt that intrigues you or that seems to relate to a card you're considering. Use the prompt as a starting point, which will give your subconscious mind a gentle push and your conscious mind something to think about.

It may help to set a timer and write without stopping for five, ten, or fifteen minutes. You could also use these writing prompts as a basis for dialogues, visualizations, or letters in your journal.

In Your Own Words

My favorite card is the [name of card] because _____.

I don't understand the [name of card] because _____.

I really dislike the [name of card] because _____.

I am just like the [name of card] because _____.

I act like the [name of card] when I _____.

Sometimes I feel like the [name of card] because _____.

This card makes me feel _____.

This card makes me think _____.

This card reminds me of _____.

If I were the [name of card], I would _____.

If I were the [name of card], I would feel _____.

If I were the [name of card], I would say _____.

If I were the [name of card], I would think _____.

If I were the [name of card], I would be _____.

The most important symbol on [name of card] is _____.

The least important symbol on [name of card] is _____.

The most striking symbol on [name of card] is _____.

At first, I didn't notice the _____ on the [name of card].

I know someone who reminds me of the [name of card]; [who? and why?]

Get into Character

I am the [name of card]. I came to you because _____.

I am the [name of card]. You chose me because _____.

I am the [name of card]. You would never guess it by looking at me, but _____.

I am the [name of card]. I often fantasize about _____.

I am the [name of card]. When I look back on my life, I regret _____.

I am the [name of card]. When I look back on my life, I am proud of _____.

I am the [name of card]. When I look back on my life, I am ashamed of _____.

I am the [name of card]. The happiest day of my life was _____.

I am the [name of card]. The greatest tragedy of my life was _____.

I am the [name of card]. I was born to _____.

I am the [name of card]. I was destined to _____.

I am the [name of card]. My biggest mistake was _____.

I am the [name of card]. If I could change anything about myself, it would be _____.

I am the [name of card]. Someday, I will _____.

I am the [name of card]. My most prized possession is my
_____.

I am the [name of card]. Spiritually, I feel _____.

I am the [name of card]. Emotionally, I feel _____.

I am the [name of card]. Physically, I feel _____.

I am the [name of card]. Intellectually, I feel _____.

I am the [name of card]. When I pray, I pray to _____.

I am the [name of card]. When I pray, I pray for _____.

I am the [name of card]. I have always loved _____.

I am the [name of card]. You need me because _____.

I am the [name of card]. You don't understand me because
_____.

I am the [name of card]. I will show you _____.

I am the [name of card]. I will teach you _____.

I am the [name of card], and I came here today to tell you that
_____.

I am the [name of card], and I have a secret. It is _____.

APPENDIX II

Minor Arcana Correspondences

	WANDS	CUPS	SWORDS	PENTACLES
PLAYING CARDS	clubs	hearts	spades	diamonds
ELEMENT	fire	water	air	earth
QUALITY	hot	cold	moist	dry
REALM	spiritual	emotional	intellectual	physical, material
EXPRESSION	action	reflection	communication, conflict	stability
JUNGIAN PSYCHOLOGY	intuition	feeling	thinking	sensation
ASTROLOGICAL SIGN	Aries, Leo, Sagittarius	Cancer, Scorpio, Pisces	Gemini, Libra, Aquarius	Taurus, Virgo, Capricorn
YIN/YANG	yang/active	yin/receptive	yang/active	yin/receptive
MALE/FEMALE	male	female	male	female
FAMILY	father	mother	son	daughter
SEASON	spring	summer	fall	winter
DIRECTION	south	west	east	north
UNIVERSE	sun	ocean, rivers	sky	land
PLANT	seeds	leaves	flowers	roots
TIME OF DAY	noon	sunset	sunrise	midnight

	WANDS	CUPS	SWORDS	PENTACLES
MEDIEVAL CLASS	farmers/ peasants	clergy	soldiers/ nobility	merchants
HUMOR	choleric	sanguine	phlegmatic	melancholic
ANIMAL	lion	serpent, eagle	man, angel	bull
ELEMENTAL CREATURE	salamander	undine	sylph	gnome
ANGEL	Raphael	Gabriel	Michael	Uriel
GOSPEL	Mark	John	Matthew	Luke
HEBREW LETTER	Yod	Heh	Vau	Heh
FUNCTION	divine spark	initial chaos	development of form	finished creation
COLOR	yellow	red	blue	green
METAL	gold, iron	quick-silver	copper, tin	lead, silver

APPENDIX III

How to Conduct a Tarot Card Reading

If you came to this book as a journaler but not a tarot reader, you might like to develop your own tarot reading routine to use in conjunction with your work. Here is a step-by-step guide to a typical tarot reading.

1. If you are reading for another person, sit directly across from each other with the cards in the middle, or sit side by side with the cards in front of you. If you are reading for yourself, find a comfortable place to sit where you won't be interrupted.

2. Clear the room of bystanders, light a candle, and calm yourself with a few moments of deep breathing or quiet contemplation.

3. Look through the deck to choose a significator—a card that depicts the question, concern, or situation you want to explore. If you like, you can follow the rule of thumb that calls for using court cards: Pages for children, Knights for adolescents and young adults, Queens for women, and Kings for men.

4. Lay the significator face up, and shuffle the rest of the deck thoroughly. Many readers shuffle the deck seven times: not only is it a mystical number, it also randomizes the cards fairly well. You can shuffle poker-style, hand over hand, or by mixing the cards in a slush pile on the table.

5. As you shuffle the cards, concentrate on your question or concern to focus the reading and imbue the cards with the essence of the issue at hand.

6. Use your left hand, which is associated with the unconscious, to cut the deck into three piles. You might want to look at the top card in each pile for a quick mini-reading: the three cards may represent the past, present, and future of the situation.

7. Put the deck back together. Take a look at the card on the bottom of the deck; it sometimes represents unconscious factors and motivations that influence a reading, or hidden or unseen forces that are at work.

8. Lay the cards out in the spread of your choosing, keeping them face down. Whether you use a simple three-card past, present, and future spread, or a more complex layout like the Celtic Cross, you should know in advance what each card position represents, and have a timeline in mind for the response.

9. Turn each card face up, one by one. Turn them from right to left, just as you would turn the pages in a book. Try to avoid flipping the cards end over end. That way, upright cards remain upright, and reversals can be easily spotted.

10. Most of the cards should be oriented toward you, so you're not looking at the images upside down. The cards should always be interpreted from the reader's point of view. (If someone is sitting across from you, you can turn them around so they can have a better look.)

11. As you turn over each card, say its name aloud, and describe the image on the card. Point out any symbolism that seems significant.

12. If a card is upside down, it may represent forces that are blocked, delayed, or misinterpreted. A reversed card might also indicate energy that is being misused or an issue that needs special attention.

13. Once all of the cards have been turned face up, go back through the spread to note a number of issues: What colors are most prominent? Which cards seem most important? Which cards seem to be looking at each other, and which ones seem isolated? Which cards seem to be coming into the spread, and which ones are leaving? Which cards are supporting the others? Which cards are saying the same things, and which ones are contradicting the others? What themes do you notice?

14. Consider how many of the cards come from the powerful Major Arcana and how many originate in the everyday Minor Arcana. Which suit is predominant? Remember that cups symbolize emotional affairs, swords represent intellectual concerns, wands stand for spiritual matters, and pentacles represent physical matters.

15. Conduct a quick count of the numbers on each card. If most of the cards in the spread have low numbers, such as aces, twos, and threes, you are just beginning a cycle. If most of the numbers are fours, fives, and sixes, you are in the thick of things. If the numbers are sevens, eights, and nines, you are near the end of a phase. Tens signify successful completion and preparation for a new cycle.

16. Court cards usually signify people in your life or aspects of your own personality that are reflected by the people around you.

17. If any card seems too confusing or unclear to interpret, lay a clarification card on top.

18. Try to end each reading on a positive note whether you're reading for yourself or for a friend. Offer a final summary of the spread, point out the factors that are within your control and any opportunities for improving the situation.

19. Once a session has concluded, record notes and comments in your tarot journal.

20. Finally, put the cards away. Some tarot readers return each card in the deck to an upright position. Some "seal" the deck by placing favorite cards on the top and bottom. Some wrap their cards in silk or place them in a special wooden box—traditionally stored above head level—to protect the cards from unwelcome psychic vibrations.

Tarot Card Keywords

*I*f you come to this book as a journaler but not a tarot card reader, you can refer to this chart of keywords to guide you in your interpretations of the cards. Many of the keywords come directly from Arthur Edward Waite's *Pictorial Key to the Tarot*.

The Major Arcana

- 0. THE FOOL. New beginnings, a leap of faith, the happy wanderer, adventure, folly, mania, delirium

- 1. THE MAGICIAN. Skill, diplomacy, self-confidence, will, mastery, showmanship, and a reminder of the esoteric maxim "As above, so below"

- 2. THE HIGH PRIESTESS. Intuition, hidden wisdom, spiritual secrets, mystery, silence

- 3. THE EMPRESS. Creativity, fertility, growth, and nature

- 4. THE EMPEROR. Civilization, stability, power, protection, authority, order, control

- 5. THE HIEROPHANT. Society, spiritual teachings, organized religion, culture, marriage, alliance, inspiration, mercy, goodness

6. THE LOVERS. Love, attraction, choices, partnerships, balance, duality

7. THE CHARIOT. Travel, movement, independence, mastery of one's drives, warrior spirit, triumph

8. STRENGTH. Courage, fortitude, self-control, power

9. THE HERMIT. Wisdom, solitude, experience, guidance, prudence, disguise

10. THE WHEEL OF FORTUNE. Destiny, fortune, success, luck, expansion, the circle of the year, cycles of life

11. JUSTICE. Fairness, balance, equity, legal matters

12. THE HANGED MAN. Isolation, sacrifice, separation, withdrawal, patience, enlightenment, initiation, new perspectives, alternate realities

13. DEATH. Endings, transitions, new beginnings, regeneration

14. TEMPERANCE. Balance, moderation, management

15. THE DEVIL. Temptation, materialism, addiction, human nature

16. THE TOWER. Disaster, calamity, ruin, catastrophe, destruction, liberation, release

17. THE STAR. Heavenly guidance, inspiration, wish fulfillment

18. THE MOON. Reflection, shadow, hidden enemies, darkness, intuition, romance, wax and wane, ebb and flow, secrets, the unconscious

19. THE SUN. Full consciousness, enlightenment, happiness, annual events

20. JUDGEMENT. Karma, destiny, responsibility, forgiveness, resurrection, new life

21. THE WORLD. Conclusions, completion, endings and new beginnings

The Minor Arcana

The Suit of Wands

ACE OF WANDS. Creativity, invention, virility, potency

TWO OF WANDS. Planning, preparation, dominion, contemplation

THREE OF WANDS. Opportunity, enterprise, effort, trade, commerce, discovery, business success, economic strength

FOUR OF WANDS. Prosperity, partnerships, haven, repose, harmony, prosperity, peace

FIVE OF WANDS. Challenges, scuffles, strife, imitation warfare, strenuous competition, struggle

SIX OF WANDS. Victory, conquest

SEVEN OF WANDS. Defiance, defense, valor, discussion, successful negotiations, competition

EIGHT OF WANDS. Communication, travel, speed, flight, arrows of love

NINE OF WANDS. Resilience, resistance, strength

TEN OF WANDS. Burden, overwork, oppression, suffering

PAGE OF WANDS. Spiritual concepts and lessons; a dark, faithful young man; a lover, an envoy, a postman

KNIGHT OF WANDS. Spiritual rescue; departure, absence, flight, emigration, a new home; a dark, friendly young man

QUEEN OF WANDS. Spiritual nurture and protection; a dark, friendly, chaste, loving, honorable woman; love of money; success in business

KING OF WANDS. The generation and administration of spiritual energy; honesty; a dark and friendly married man

The Suit of Cups

ACE OF CUPS. New love, overflowing emotion, fertility, joy, nourishment, abundance

TWO OF CUPS. Attraction, commitment, love

THREE OF CUPS. Friendship, celebration, abundance, merriment, solace, healing

FOUR OF CUPS. Disenchantment, boredom, weariness, disgust, aversion

FIVE OF CUPS. Sorrow, loss

SIX OF CUPS. Nostalgia, pleasure

SEVEN OF CUPS. Choices, daydreams, illusions

EIGHT OF CUPS. Seeking, quests, crusades, abandonment

NINE OF CUPS. Pleasure, contentment, drunkenness, material or physical happiness

TEN OF CUPS. Contentment, perfect happiness, success, happy home and family

PAGE OF CUPS. Emotional lessons and messages; a student; reflection and meditation

KNIGHT OF CUPS. Emotional rescue; arrival, approach, advances, propositions, invitations

QUEEN OF CUPS. Emotional nurture and protection; dreamy, visionary; a good, fair, honest, and devoted woman; success, happiness, pleasure, wisdom, virtue; a perfect spouse and a good mother

KING OF CUPS. The generation and administration of emotional energy; a fair man, an intelligent man; a man of business, law, or divinity; responsibility

The Suit of Swords

ACE OF SWORDS. Inspiration, clarity, conception, pregnancy

TWO OF SWORDS. Difficult decisions, peace restored, courage, concord

THREE OF SWORDS. Heartache, sorrow

FOUR OF SWORDS. Recuperation, retreat, rest from strife, repose, exile

FIVE OF SWORDS. Poor sportsmanship, defeat, degradation, infamy, dishonor, loss

SIX OF SWORDS. Travel by water, solace, reward

SEVEN OF SWORDS. Dishonesty, thievery, betrayal, futility

EIGHT OF SWORDS. Restrictions, cruelty, victimhood

NINE OF SWORDS. Insomnia, nightmares, despair, cruelty, lamentation

TEN OF SWORDS. Overkill, martyrdom, ruin, desolation, sadness

PAGE OF SWORDS. Intellectual concepts and lessons; secret service, vigilance, stealth, a spy

KNIGHT OF SWORDS. Intellectual rescue; chivalry, skill, bravery, defense, war

QUEEN OF SWORDS. The nurture and protection of intellectual energy; a sharp-tongued woman, a widow, a woman with a keen wit and intelligence

KING OF SWORDS. The generation and administration of intellectual energy; justice, the power of life and death; command, authority, militant intelligence

The Suit of Pentacles

ACE OF PENTACLES. Physical and material foundations

TWO OF PENTACLES. Balance, juggling of resources, harmonious change

THREE OF PENTACLES. Artistic and spiritual mastery

FOUR OF PENTACLES. Miserliness, stinginess, isolation, earthly power

FIVE OF PENTACLES. Poverty, loss, material trouble

SIX OF PENTACLES. Charity, generosity, material success, gift-giving

SEVEN OF PENTACLES. The wait before the harvest, success unfulfilled, barter, innocence

EIGHT OF PENTACLES. Apprenticeship, industry, prudence, work, employment, commission, craftsmanship, skill

NINE OF PENTACLES. Comfort, abundance, material gain, prudence, safety, success, accomplishment, discernment

TEN OF PENTACLES. Wealth, gain, riches, family matters, archives, family home

PAGE OF PENTACLES. Physical lessons; study, scholarship, reflection, management

KNIGHT OF PENTACLES. Offers physical rescue; slowness, heaviness, endurance, utility, serviceability, responsibility

QUEEN OF PENTACLES. Nurtures and protects physical energy; a dark, intelligent woman with a great soul; opulence, generosity, magnificence, security, liberty

KING OF PENTACLES. Generates and administers physical energy; a dark man; courage, valor, intelligence, business aptitude, mathematical gifts

APPENDIX V
Forms and Templates

You can find downloadable, print-friendly versions of the following forms and templates online at the following address: www.tarotjournaling.com.

What's In the Cards?

Remember today's insights with this record of your tarot reading.

DATE _____ PLACE _____

DECK _____ SPREAD _____

QUESTION OR CONCERN _____

_____

_____

Reading Summary

Each card's meaning is highlighted by the position in which it falls.

SIGNIFICATOR _____

COVERING/SITUATION _____

CROSSING/OBSTACLES _____

CROWNING/HIGHEST GOOD _____

FOUNDATION _____

PAST _____

FUTURE _____

SELF _____

OTHERS _____

HOPES AND FEARS _____

MOST LIKELY OUTCOME _____

NOTES AND COMMENTS _____

_____

_____

CONCLUSION _____

_____

_____

Suit Yourself

What do the four suits represent? Here's a quick guide:

Wands: spiritual issues
Cups: emotional affairs
Swords: intellectual matters
Pentacles: material things

Major Players

Major Arcana cards represent powerful forces in your life.

❑ 0. The Fool
❑ 1. The Magician
❑ 2. The High Priestess
❑ 3. The Empress
❑ 4. The Emperor
❑ 5. The Hierophant
❑ 6. The Lovers
❑ 7. The Chariot
❑ 8. Justice
❑ 9. The Hermit
❑ 10. Wheel of Fortune
❑ 11. Strength
❑ 12. The Hanged Man
❑ 13. Death
❑ 14. Temperance
❑ 15. The Devil
❑ 16. The Tower
❑ 17. The Star
❑ 18. The Moon
❑ 19. The Sun
❑ 20. Judgement
❑ 21. The World

Tarot by the Numbers

Aces: new beginnings
2: duality and balance
3: blending and growth
4: solid foundations
5: upsetting the balance
6: re-establishing the balance
7: new awareness
8: re-evaluation
9: near completion
10: completion, prepare to begin again
Pages: lessons, news, messages
Knights: adventures, protection
Queens: safeguard, nurture
Kings: organization, defense

Minor Keys

You control the forces of the Minor Arcana.

	Wands	Cups	Swords	Pentacles
Ace				
Two				
Three				
Four				
Five				
Six				
Seven				
Eight				
Nine				
Ten				
Page				
Knight				
Queen				
King				

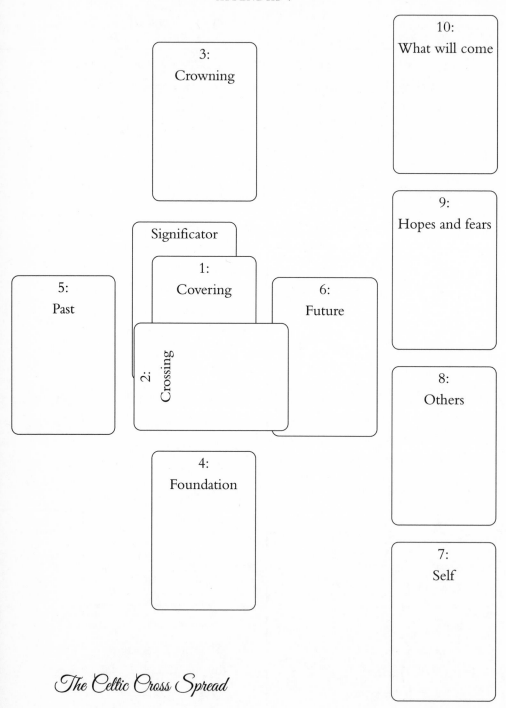

The Celtic Cross Spread

The Card-a-Day Record

Draw one card a day for yourself. Keep a record of the cards you draw, and look for patterns and distribution over time.

CARD	DATE	DATE	DATE	DATE	DATE
Fool					
Magician					
High Priestess					
Empress					
Emperor					
Hierophant					
Lovers					
Chariot					
Strength					
Hermit					
Wheel of Fortune					
Justice					
Hanged Man					
Death					
Temperance					
Devil					
Tower					
Star					
Moon					
Sun					
Judgement					
World					

CARD	DATE	DATE	DATE	DATE	DATE
Ace of Wands					
Two of Wands					
Three of Wands					
Four of Wands					
Five of Wands					
Six of Wands					
Seven of Wands					
Eight of Wands					
Nine of Wands					
Ten of Wands					
Page of Wands					
Knight of Wands					
Queen of Wands					
King of Wands					
Ace of Cups					
Two of Cups					
Three of Cups					
Four of Cups					
Five of Cups					
Six of Cups					
Seven of Cups					
Eight of Cups					
Nine of Cups					
Ten of Cups					
Page of Cups					
Knight of Cups					
Queen of Cups					
King of Cups					

CARD	DATE	DATE	DATE	DATE	DATE
Ace of Swords					
Two of Swords					
Three of Swords					
Four of Swords					
Five of Swords					
Six of Swords					
Seven of Swords					
Eight of Swords					
Nine of Swords					
Ten of Swords					
Page of Swords					
Knight of Swords					
Queen of Swords					
King of Swords					
Ace of Pentacles					
Two of Pentacles					
Three of Pentacles					
Four of Pentacles					
Five of Pentacles					
Six of Pentacles					
Seven of Pentacles					
Eight of Pentacles					
Nine of Pentacles					
Ten of Pentacles					
Page of Pentacles					
Knight of Pentacles					
Queen of Pentacles					
King of Pentacles					

Bibliography

Adams, Kathleen. *Journal to the Self: Twenty-Two Paths to Personal Growth.* New York: Warner Books, 1990.

Amberstone, Wald, and Ruth Ann Amberstone. *The Tarot School Correspondence Course.* www.tarotschool.com.

Ando, Arnell. *Transformational Tarot.* Stamford, Connecticut: U.S. Games Systems, Inc., 2006.

Baldwin, Christina. *One to One: Self-Understanding through Journal Writing.* New York: M. Evans and Co., Inc., 1977.

————. *Life's Companion: Journal Writing as a Spiritual Quest.* New York: Bantam Books, 1990.

Bender, Sheila. *A Year in the Life: Journaling for Self-Discovery.* Cincinnati, Ohio: Walking Stick Press, 2000.

Bunning, Joan. *Learning the Tarot: A Tarot Book for Beginners.* York Beach, Maine: Red Wheel/Weiser, 1998.

Cameron, Julia. *The Artist's Way: A Spiritual Path to Higher Creativity.* New York: Tarcher, 1992.

Conway, D. J., and Lisa Hunt. *The Celtic Dragon Tarot.* St. Paul, Minnesota: Llewellyn Publications, 1999.

Dickerman, Alexandra Collins. *Following Your Path: Using Myths, Symbols, and Images to Explore Your Inner Life.* New York: Jeremy P. Tarcher/Putnam, 1992.

Epel, Naomi. *The Observation Deck: A Tool Kit for Writers.* San Francisco: Chronicle Books, 1998.

Fairfield, Gail, and Patti Provo. *Inspiration Tarot: A Workbook for Understanding and Creating Your Own Tarot Deck.* York Beach, Maine: Samuel Weiser, Inc., 1991.

Ferguson, Anna-Marie. *Legend: The Arthurian Tarot.* St. Paul, Minnesota: Llewellyn Publications, 1997.

Franklin, Anna, and Paul Mason. *The Fairy Ring.* St. Paul, Minnesota: Llewellyn Publications, 2002.

Geiss, Charlene, and Claudia Jessup. *Inner Outings: The Diarist's Deck of 33 Cards and Book of Exploration.* Novato, California: New World Library, 2002.

Goldberg, Natalie. *Writing Down the Bones: Freeing the Writer Within.* Boston: Shambhala, 1986.

Greene, Liz, and Juliet Sharman-Burke. *The Mythic Tarot.* New York: Fireside, 2001.

Greenberg, Martin H., and Lawrence Schimel. *Tarot Fantastic: Sixteen spellbinding tales of those who dared to learn their futures through the magic of the cards.* New York: Daw Books, 1997.

Greer, Mary K. *Tarot for Your Self: A Workbook for Personal Transformation.* North Hollywood, California: Newcastle Publishing Co., Inc., 1984.

Guarino, Louis. *Writing Your Authentic Self.* New York: Dell Publishing, 1999.

Holzer, Burghild Nina. *A Walk Between Heaven and Earth: A Personal Journal on Writing and the Creative Process.* New York: Bell Tower, 1994.

Johnson, Alexandra. *Leaving a Trace: On Keeping a Journal.* New York: Little, Brown and Company, 2001.

Keen, Sam, and Anne Valley-Fox. *Your Mythic Journey: Finding Meaning in Your Life Through Writing and Storytelling.* New York: Penguin Putnam Inc., 1973.

Kenner, Corrine. *The Epicurean Tarot.* Stamford, Connecticut: U.S. Games Systems, Inc., 2001.

Landvik, Lorna. *Welcome to the Great Mysterious.* New York: Ballantine Books, 2002.

Louis, Anthony. *Tarot Plain and Simple.* St. Paul, Minnesota: Llewellyn Publications, 1996.

McElroy, Mark. *Putting the Tarot to Work.* St. Paul, Minnesota: Llewellyn Publications, 2004.

Metzger, Deena. *Writing for Your Life: A Guide and Companion to the Inner Worlds.* New York: HarperCollins Publishers, 1992.

Michelsen, Teresa. *The Complete Tarot Reader: Everything You Need to Know from Start to Finish.* St. Paul, Minnesota: Llewellyn Publications, 2005.

Neubauer, Joan R. *The Complete Idiot's Guide to Journaling.* Indianapolis, Indiana: Alpha Books, 2001.

———. *Dear Diary: The Art and Craft of Writing a Creative Journal.* Orem, Utah: Ancestry Publishing, 2002.

Ondaatje, Michael. *The English Patient.* New York: Vintage, 1993.

Pennebaker, James W. *Opening Up: The Healing Power of Expressing Emotions.* New York: Guilford Press, 1997.

Pollack, Rachel, and Caitlin Matthews. *Tarot Tales.* New York: Ace Books, 1996.

Rainer, Tristine. *The New Diary: How to Use a Journal for Self-Guidance and Expanded Creativity.* New York: Penguin Putnam Inc., 1978.

———. *Your Life as Story: Discovering the "New Autobiography" and Writing Memoir as Literature.* New York: Penguin Putnam Inc., 1998.

Ravenwolf, Silver, and Nigel Jackson. *The Witches Runes.* St. Paul, Minnesota: Llewellyn Publications, 1996.

Schneider, Myra, and John Killick. *Writing for Self-Discovery: A Personal Approach to Creative Writing.* Element Books Limited, 1998.

Sexton, David. *The Tarot of Oz.* St. Paul, Minnesota: Llewellyn Publications, 2002.

Sheldon, Mary, and Christopher Stone. *The Meditation Journal: 28 Spiritual Growth Exercises to Inspire Inner Peace, Self-Awareness, and Happiness.* West Hollywood, California: Dove Books, 1996.

Smyth, Joshua M. Smyth, Ph.D., Arthur A. Stone, Ph.D., Adam Hurewitz, M.D., and Alan Kaell, M.D. "Effects of Writing About Stressful Experiences on Symptom Reduction in Patients with Asthma or Rheumatoid Arthritis; A Randomized Trial," *Journal of the American Medical Association,* April 14, 1999: Vol. 281, No. 14, p.1304.

Waite, Arthur Edward. *The Pictorial Key to the Tarot.* Stamford, Connecticut: U.S. Games Systems, Inc., 1992.

Weldon, Michele. *Writing to Save Your Life: How to Honor Your Story Through Journaling.* Center City, Minnesota: Hazelden, 2001.

Tall Dark Stranger
Tarot for Love and Romance

Corrine Kenner

For centuries, the love-struck, lovesick, and lovelorn have consulted the tarot—a tradition still thriving today. *Tall Dark Stranger* makes it easy for anyone to explore matters of the heart through tarot. There is even a guide to tarot terms and symbols.

Corrine Kenner's tour of the tarot begins with its colorful, romantic history. She goes on to describe the deck itself—explaining its structure, suits, symbolism, archetypes, and astrological associations—while relating its special significance in love and relationships. The second part of the book is devoted to the nitty-gritty of tarot readings: choosing a deck, preparing for a reading, asking appropriate questions, timing events, and interpreting cards and spreads. By the end of the book, readers will have a powerful edge in conquering the ever-mysterious ways of love.

0-7387-0548-9
312 pp., 7½ x 9⅛, illus. $15.95

Taking the Tarot to Heart
*Fun & Creative Ways to Improve
Your Love Life*

Mark McElroy

*W*aiting for Prince Charming may not be an effective strategy for finding love, just as ignoring relationship problems isn't always the best solution. Instead of letting chance rule romance, Mark McElroy suggests using the tarot to improve your love life.

No knowledge of the tarot or belief in the supernatural is necessary. Anyone can use *Taking the Tarot to Heart* to take charge of their romantic destiny. For both singles and couples, this book provides tarot spreads and exercises to answer questions like "How can I find my soulmate?" and "How can I spice up my love life?" Emphasizing the practical, not the mystical, McElroy demonstrates how easy it is to find creative solutions to relationship issues without bleeding the mystery and meaning out of romance. Many topics are covered: defining your perfect partner, dating, gifts, break-ups, granting forgiveness, and more.

0-7387-0536-5
264 pp., 7½ x 9⅛, illus. $16.95

Putting the Tarot to Work
Creative Problem Solving, Effective Decision Making, and Personal Career Planning

Mark McElroy

*Y*ou have your cell phone, your pager, and your palm pilot. But a tarot deck? Why not? It's the perfect tool for thinking outside the box.

Business manager and consultant Mark McElroy has worked and thrived in the corporate pressure cooker. Let him show you the secrets of using the cards to boost your creativity, make better decisions, and increase your value as a boss or employee. Apply this versatile tool today to clarify your values, define your goals, and restore meaning to your career. The cards can even help you plan productive meetings, breathe new life into dull presentations, and improve business relationships.

0-7387-0444-X
264 pp., 7½ x 9⅛ $16.95

The Complete Tarot Reader
Everything You Need to Know from Start to Finish

Teresa C. Michelsen

*T*eresa Michelsen's one-of-a-kind self-study program helps students develop a long-lasting, intuitive approach to tarot reading that works with any tarot deck! Instead of memorizing standard card meanings and spreads, readers are encouraged to use their own life experiences and knowledge to craft a personal understanding of the cards.

Organized like a study guide, this book includes study goals, progress activities, and easy exercises for exploring the suits, court cards, major arcana, and a variety of reading techniques, including methods to work with reversals, dignities, timed readings, and large spreads. Michelsen also discusses the underlying structures and patterns in the tarot and how various cards are related to astrology, numerology, psychology, and myth. Practical aspects of tarot reading—difficult clients, reader's block, good questions, and ethical issues—are also covered.

0-7387-0434-2
288 pp., 7½ x 9⅛, illus. $15.95

To Write to the Author

If you wish to contact the author or would like more information about this book, please write to the author in care of Llewellyn Worldwide and we will forward your request. Both the author and publisher appreciate hearing from you and learning of your enjoyment of this book and how it has helped you. Llewellyn Worldwide cannot guarantee that every letter written to the author can be answered, but all will be forwarded. Please write to:

Corrine Kenner
℅ Llewellyn Worldwide
2143 Wooddale Drive, Dept. 0-7387-0643-4
Woodbury, MN 55125-2989

Please enclose a self-addressed stamped envelope for reply,
or $1.00 to cover costs. If outside U.S.A., enclose
international postal reply coupon.

Many of Llewellyn's authors have websites with additional information and resources. For more information, please visit our website:

www.llewellyn.com